Persistence Pays

How getting what you want is easier than you think

Persistency Pays

How getting what you want is easier than you think

By Lori Raudnask

Published by:

Motivated Publishing Ventures

ISBN: 978-0-9784415-5-5

Printed in Canada and USA

First Edition: April 2008

Edited by: MR, RAS, MPVP

Cover design: Beth Smith

Photography: Paul Sontrop

Book layout by: RAS

Project Management: Rod Schulhauser

Zdenka

Thanks for sharing this special day! It means a lot.

Love,

Lori Raudiask

my

I will persist and not give up until I succeed.

motto

PS You are so persistent in everything you do!

Dedication

I dedicate this book to my supportive and wonderful husband Lembit. I could not have done this without you! Also to my very special children, Megan and Kyle, who are the pride and joy in my life. Thank you for putting up with the long hours it took to bring this book to life and letting me leave for days at a time to write. Thanks for your encouragement and inspiration that allowed me to pursue greater dreams. Your love and support are the true wealth of my life. You have encouraged me to be the best that I can be, and most importantly, to share what I have learned with others.

Acknowledgements

I would like to thank God for blessing me with the gifts of writing, speaking and helping others achieve success. I pray this book will help people go after what they want and persist to reach their dreams, to really go after what they want. I would like to thank all the teachers and leaders who have taught me so much — I have been blessed in my life to have had the best teachers. I would like to acknowledge Glenn Butler who was my mentor and really showed me how to reach for the stars. I'd like to thank the thousands of people who have been my customers and have supported my business over the years. Without you I would not have had the opportunity to grow and experience the joy that sales has brought to my life. Thanks also to my dear friends and family who have supported me through this journey. And to my mom and dad, without you I wouldn't be where I am today. Thank you for always being there.

A special thank you to Rod for your excitement about this project and for your guidance in helping me bring out my best ideas and publish my first book.

Introduction

What is closing? At what point in life do we really start closing? When was the last time you saw a child close? I was just at the grocery store and witnessed the perfect closing. Picture this, a child is in the cart and spots the chocolate bars on a shelf. After glancing over at his mom, the child lets out a blood curdling scream. The mother rushes over to see what is wrong and notices that the child is pointing towards the chocolate bars. The mom sternly says, "No, you can not have that" ,and within seconds the screams go up a few notches in volume. A few embarrassing moments later, mom reaches across and hands the child a chocolate bar. There you have it, results achieved, the close was made!

At what point in school do you start closing? Picture this, you are at a school dance and you see the girl of your dreams across the gym and a slow song begins to play. You fix your hair, straighten your shirt, take a deep breath and muster up the nerve to start slowly walking across the gymnasium. All the while your hands are sweating and you are sure everyone can see your heart pounding out of your shirt. You get to the girl, smile and say something silly while wanting to smack yourself in the head. Then finally you find the courage and ask her if she wants to dance. She smiles at you and gently says, "sure." The close is made.

At what point during the job interview do you close? Is it the point where you fill out the application or when you shake the interviewer's hand? Or, is it when you get the job?

In business and in life, we need to always be thinking about closing. It starts from a very early age. But what comes with the act of closing is the act of being persistent. Persistence pays and the more persistent you are the more you close.

Persistence Pays and the more persistent you are the more you close.

This book will appeal to people of all ages because selling is a way of life; and the earlier you learn to sell yourself the better you will be able to close. It doesn't matter if you are going for a job interview, running for school council or selling a million dollar product, the biggest sale is the one you make to yourself. Once you can sell to yourself with the persistence of practice, you can sell to anyone.

As you read this book, real life situations are outlined that show making a sale is not difficult. The hardest part is simply making the decision that you are going to sell. It is having the vision for what you want to accomplish and then going for it. In my 30 years of sales experience it really isn't the product that has made me successful; it is my passion for what I am doing. It is the passion for helping people get what they want and need. If you have the passion the money will follow. Too often people are focused on the money and that is where they fall short. Focus on what you can do for others and how you can help them and you will see the money flow in. Don't be afraid to show your passion for what you do. You never know what you can accomplish until you try. The opportunities are endless and you just have to go for it. If you don't accomplish what you set out to do, that is ok, just try again. Be persistent and it will pay off.

Remember, opportunity awaits,

Lori Raudnask

"The golden opportunity you are seeking is in yourself. It is not in your environment; it is not in luck or chance, or the help of others, it is in yourself alone.

There are powers inside of you which, if you could discover and use, would make of you everything you ever dreamed or imagined you could become."

Orison Swett Marden

Contents

Acknowledgements....vii
Introduction....xi

Part I: Mindset

Chapter 1 Mindset Introduction....1
Chapter 2 Persistence....5
Chapter 3 Be a Willing Student....13
Chapter 4 An Ant's Determination....17
Chapter 5 What Does it Mean to be Relentless....21
Chapter 6 Create a Visual Picture....23
Chapter 7 How to Anchor Your Victories....27
Chapter 8 Go Red....29
Chapter 9 Results Rather Than Status....31
Chapter 10 Momentum....35

Part 2: Skill Set

Chapter 11 Skill Set Introduction....39
Chapter 12 The 15 Most Critical Words in Your Sales Vocabulary....43
Chapter 13 Learn From Your Mistakes....49
Chapter 14 Learn to Motivate Yourself....53
Chapter 15 Accountability....59
Chapter 16 Look Like You Mean Business....65
Chapter 17 Get Out of Your Own Way....67
Chapter 18 Why Network?....69
Chapter 19 Patterning Your Success....75
Chapter 20 Step 1 - Who....77
Chapter 21 Step 2 - Connect....79
Chapter 22 Step 3 - Present....87
Chapter 23 Step 4 - Close....93
Chapter 24 Step 5 - Follow Up....99
Chapter 25 Step 6 - Follow Through....103

Contents

Chapter 26 Step 7 - Generate More Business.............107
Chapter 27 Step 8 - Repeat the Pattern.....................111
Chapter 28 Are You Ready to Break Out of Your Shell?..115
Chapter 29 Learning is a Skill.....................................119
Chapter 30 What Not to Say in Sales..........................121
Chapter 31 Can you Really Make a Sale Anywhere?.......................................125
Chapter 32 Attributes of a Successful Person in Sales.......................................127

Part 3: Action
Chapter 33 Action Introduction..................................133
Chapter 34 Have a Plan of Action.............................141
Chapter 35 Are You Really Giving Your Best?.............143
Chapter 36 Do You Watch Things Happen?................147
Chapter 37 Have You Ever Gotten Detoured?............151
Chapter 38 Discipline, Practice and Accountability...155
Chapter 39 Getting Your Business off the Ground.......159
Chapter 40 If You are Going to Fall, Fall Forward........161
Chapter 41 If You Knew You Could Not Fail... What Would You Do?.............................165
Chapter 42 Being Consistent....................................169
Chapter 43 It Takes 21 Days to Change a Habit!........173
Chapter 44 Raise Your Game...................................177
Chapter 45 Sales Are Not Always About What You Like to Do...............................181
Chapter 46 Taking Initiative in Sales...........................187
Chapter 47 How to Rev Yourself Up in Your Business....191

Conclusion...195

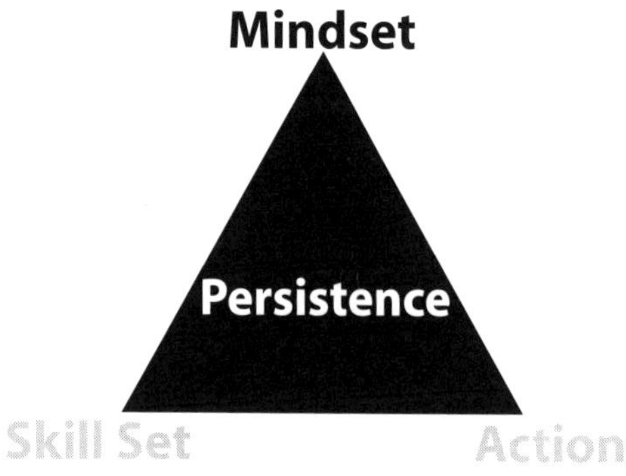

Mindset
Persistence
Skill Set
Action

PART 1
Mindset

Chapter 1

Mindset Introduction

"If you can dream it, you can do it."
Walt Disney

The mind is incredible. Take a minute to think about something that you really, really want. Is it a new pair of shoes, is it a new job, is it a relationship, is it a certain weight you would like to be, is it closing that deal you have been working on for months? Once a thought comes into your mind your brain is engaged. Now, we can take that thought and dismiss it or we can take that thought and do something about it. You are, in fact, the boss of your own brain. Everything we do or accomplish is up to us as individuals. What do you really want? First, you have to make that decision. Our mindset can take us as far as we want to go. If we listen to ourselves and go after what we want, we have made the first step towards our potential.

The mind can hold us back too; when we say things like "I can't do that" or "I can never afford that" or "I'll never get that job."

I was hosting a training conference call recently. The group on the call was in a slump. It was the middle of winter and since the sun hadn't been shining much lately there seemed to be a winter-blues theme happening. As we talked about why they were not getting out there, making sales calls and trying to increase their business, it dawned on me what the problem was. They needed to change what they were doing. They needed to change their negative mindset to a positive one.

We began to talk about what would happen if we changed our mindset to make it a positive one. We would generate positive change in all aspects of our lives; it would cause a ripple effect to our family, our mood and our work place. But here is the clincher, why are we afraid to change? What holds us back from change? Why do we allow fear to hold us back? Why does fear of change keep us in a rut?

One of the ladies on the call had just survived breast cancer. She said that she made a lot of changes when she was faced with this crisis but now that things are back to normal and she is feeling great, she has fallen back into the same old rut. I told her she is not alone and that so many of us are scared of change. We allow fear to hold us back and keep us in that rut.

We allow fear to hold us back and keep us in a rut.

What we need to remember is that change is natural. Look at the seasons that change automatically. Things are either growing or dying. We change our clothing season to season, animals change their coat — change happens all around us. Therefore, you have a choice to make a change. You don't need to wait for a crisis to make a change and you don't need to wait for a season to change. Before the doctor diagnoses you with diabetes, you can change your diet. You can improve your marriage before it is too late. You can practice your presentation before your meeting. You can change your mindset and make those 10 calls each day.

Change can be very exciting and rewarding but it has to start with one person and that is YOU. Change your mindset and you change your results.

Chapter 2

Persistence

As an entrepreneur, as each year comes to an end, I always look back and see what has transpired in my business and in my life. It is a time of reflection and a time to debrief what worked and what did not work over the past year. What did I learn, and what did I learn about myself?

Have you ever had one of those moments when you stopped and really asked yourself, "What just happened and what was the lesson?" Recently I was driving down the highway in the middle lane and suddenly rubber from a truck's tire came flying towards my car. I couldn't veer to the left nor the right, as cars lined both sides of my vehicle. With a big thud, the rubber hit my car and luckily I was able to maintain control of my car as I swerved. I pulled over and to my astonishment the whole lower front of my BMW was gone! The lights were literally ripped out, my license plate was gone and the bumper was a mess. Now, I must tell you that I had just gotten my car back a week earlier from having the side painted due to vandalism. My heart sunk as I dialed my cell phone to call the police. The officer on the other end asked if I was okay and she said she would dispatch an officer to the scene.

When the officer arrived he asked for my license plate number. When I said PERSIST he chuckled and asked where the name came from. I told him I was in sales and that you always need to PERSIST to make your dreams come true. I told him I would really like to get my plate back and he said there would be a slim chance of finding it on the highway. He took my information and returned to his car. A little while later the officer returned with a smile on his face. He said he couldn't help going back to the highway to look for my plate. Even though it was dark he persisted until he found it off in the field beside the highway. I was shocked that he took the time to do this. As he handed me my crumpled PERSIST license plate, which had been run over numerous times, I said, "Thank you", and shook his hand. Before he left I handed him my business card and said, "If you have any Christmas gifts to buy and would like jewellery, give me a call and I will look after you." He then said, "Well Lori you sure are persistent, I will give you a call".

So what worked? I did not get hurt and someone went out of their way when I least expected it. The next day I wrote a letter of appreciation to the police department for the way the officer handled the accident.

What didn't work? I had to pay for another paint job and repairs. Was there any way that I could have avoided the accident?

What did I learn? How we react to any situation can determine if it has a positive or negative outcome.

What did I learn about myself? No matter what the situation, the learning can be greater than the experience itself.

A few weeks later I did get a call from the officer and he came to my open house and purchased some beautiful items for friends and family. I went the extra mile and offered to gift wrap them for him. He left the packages with me and came back a few days later to pick them up. I took a lot of time to wrap them beautifully and he was thrilled when he saw the finished product and offered to pay extra for the great wrapping job. I said absolutely not, it was my pleasure. Now, do you think I will gain new customers as a result of this sale? Absolutely!

We know that we can never stop bad things from happening to us, but we can turn our bad experiences into good ones. While at the time we may not see the lesson, we must trust that all will lead to good. If you have lost your job, you may land the job of your dreams, it may be a time of growth. A business deal that went wrong may mean that a bigger and better deal is down the road. We just have to tune our mind set that everything leads to good, if we choose so.

"Everything leads to good, " if we choose so.

I kept my crumpled up license plate and still have it in my office. When I feel like things aren't going my way I just look at the dents and bangs and the word PERSIST and it gives me that boost of energy that I need.

My energy booster!

What can you use in your life to boost your energy? If you don't have anything, go and find something. There are great plaques out there that offer inspiration. My office is filled with them and I will share a few that I have hanging up:

> *"Passion...nothing in the world has ever been accomplished without passion."*
>
> *"80% of success is showing up."*
>
> *"Success is not a destination that you ever reach. Success is the quality of your journey."*
>
> *"If you can imagine it... You can achieve it. Dream it... and you can become it."* W.A. Ward

"Do not follow where the path may lead. Go instead where there is no path and leave a trail."
Ralph Waldo Emerson

My personal favorite,

"You can't scare me, I have kids."

The future can always be brighter with a new vision.

Surround yourself with positive energy!

What if your results were not what you wanted — and no matter what you did, you just could not seem to get ahead? The future can always be brighter with a new vision.

Activity:

Take out a piece of paper and a pen now and just sit for a minute. Take time to write down 5-10 accomplishments that you had in the past year. You will begin to see what you have accomplished and will be amazed at what you really have done. Ask yourself:

- What worked?
- What didn't work?
- What do you need to do in the future to have greater wins?

If something isn't working for you, stop doing it, or come up with another plan of action. If your sales aren't at the target you set out, ask yourself:

- Why?
- Did you keep your statistics on a daily, weekly, monthly or yearly basis?

- Did you partake in personal development in the past year?
- Did you read any inspirational books?
- Did you plan your days and follow through with your plans?
- Did you focus on money instead of what your service or product can do for others?

As you reflect back, take time to congratulate yourself on what you really did accomplish, appreciate how far you have come. High-five yourself and say, WELL DONE! Remember to celebrate all victories, you truly deserve it.

Persistence is one of my favorite words. Years ago I ran a contest for my sales team. The winners got to attend a Bob Proctor seminar in Buffalo, New York. At this seminar Bob said one thing that really changed the way we thought. He said, *"If you really want something, go out and buy it. Once you have it you will be able to pay for it. Now I don't mean to go out and buy a million dollar home if you have a $100,000 budget. But if you have always dreamed of having something special, just go and get it and you will make enough sales to keep it!"* Well, that was all my husband needed to hear. We had been married five years and ever since I met him he had a picture of his dream boat on his bulletin board. The next season we were at the boat show purchasing a brand new 22' Sea Ray express cruiser. At that time the cost was $70,000....which was the price of our first home! While we were signing the papers, our hands were shaking with fear and excitement all at the same time. While we were brainstorming possible names for our boat the word "persistence" came to me. I said to my husband, "Well, we are both in sales and in sales you have to be persistent. If we weren't persistent we wouldn't have the means to buy this boat." We have changed our boat three times since then and our current boat's name is *Persistence Pays*.

When I turned 40 my mom wanted to buy me something special and she gave me money to buy my personalized license plates. I called to inquire about a few names that I had in mind. When I asked the lady if "persist" was available, she laughed and said, "Oh, I doubt it." To our surprise, "persist" had yet to be taken. This is where that crumpled license plate came from.

Bob was right; we can have what we want. What I have learned is to be persistent and go after what I want. A recently released movie you may have heard of titled, "The Secret" featured Bob Proctor. In this movie, he talks about the power of intention. He was teaching power of intention 18 years ago when I went to see him and I am grateful for that experience. Ever since I attended the conference I have been using this technique in my sales career. When I go out to sell, I always have the intention of what dollar amount I want to sell. For example, if I want to buy something, let's say a new couch, I break down how many sales I need to make in order to purchase the couch.

By never giving up, we can see the power of determination.

By never giving up, we can see the power of determination. The way you think with your mind is so powerful. For example:

If you think you can, you can. If you think you are fat, you are. If you think you are thin, you are. If you think you are ugly, you are. If you think you are beautiful, you are. If you think you suck at sales, you do. If you think you are the greatest sales person in the world, you are.

Sales people are beautiful! But, what is beauty? It is how you feel on the inside that projects on the outside. It is about what you are going to do. You are what you think you are.

If you want to accomplish it, you can accomplish it. BUT do you really want to? If you don't want it, you won't get it!

Who are you? What do you really want? Take out a piece of paper and write those two questions down. That is the easy part. Now, answer the questions. Spend some time really thinking about what you really want. Most people that I train do not know what they want. How can you get where you want to go if you don't know where it is you want to go?

One of the most important qualities you will need to develop in order to continue taking action towards your goals and dreams, is persistence.

You must be persistent in your disciplines and habits. Persist when you face challenges and adversity and be determined to achieve your dreams — no matter what! There will be many times when you will want to quit, give up and go back to doing something else. However, the one quality that will guarantee your success is the willingness to stick with it, to see it through to the end and refusing to settle for anything less than your dream. The longer you hang in there, the greater the chance that something will happen in your favor. No matter how hard it seems, the longer you persist, the more likely your success will be.

Disappointment is inevitable no matter how well you plan and how well you execute your plan. Sometimes you will be faced with odds that are overwhelming. And sometimes the universe will test your commitment to the goal you are pursuing. This can be true both personally and in business.

Sometimes the universe will test your commitment to the goal you are pursuing.

Recently I have been working with a client who has cancelled on me two times. As I was writing this part of the book the phone rang… The client tried to cancel for a third time. This time, however, I decided to get to the root of the problem. The problem incorporated both staff and personal problems the owner was going through. I had been planning to do a session on "Building a Code of Honor" for this particular business. This was the perfect time to come in and present "Code of Honor" to them. Yes, some employees may decide to leave during challenging times, but these may be the one's that are creating the challenges. By using objection handling, we were able to continue with the original training date. Sometimes when clients want to cancel on us, we use the "easy way out" and just say ok. If we persist and show we are really committed to our customers, a cancellation can be deflected.

When we are hit with obstacles, we need to think of ways to get around them. We can choose to go around, over or through the obstacle. One way or another we can do it. Really think about how to deal with the obstacle rather than giving up. Think of the solution to the obstacle. Persist until you find a way to get over, through or around it.

I Googled the word "persist" and these are the definitions that I was presented with:

> - to continue steadfastly or firmly in some state, purpose, course of action
> - to last or endure tenaciously
> - to be insistent in a statement, request, question
> - be persistent, refuse to stop
> - to keep doing, thinking, etc. in spite of opposition or difficulty; to continue asking, persuading, etc.

Persistence is constant — not a once in a while thing.

Persistence is constant — not a once in a while thing. It is critical in a winning mindset and separates intentions from success!

It will not be easy, but you will succeed if you persist.

Chapter 3

Be a Willing Student

Where are you right now? Are you still the same person you've been for the last several years? Do you have the intention to become something bigger and better than where you are right now? Perhaps you've thought about making changes and then forgotten to implement them. It is not too late to make changes NOW. It happens when? They happen when you are willing to change, forget your fears and focus on your future. Change happens NOW!

On the first print day of each New Year, our local paper dedicates the front page to the brave individuals who jump into Lake Ontario on New Year's Day. The water is freezing. Every year the Polar Bear Club meets, drops their clothing, and runs into the frigid water wearing only their bathing suits, no wet suits or insulated shoes to protect their feet. They just do it. I love to look at this picture every year and often wonder why they do it. This year I interviewed a member of the club and asked that very question. The answer intrigued me and I want to share it with you.

Leona told me that she has been a member of the club for five years now. She wanted to start the New Year fresh by taking the plunge. She was making a statement to herself, her family and God that she was ready to take a leap of faith, not only in her personal life, but in her professional career as well.

This year she said that she was no longer going to allow fear to hold her back. She wanted to create positive energy in her life and she wasn't going to allow fear to paralyze her for a moment longer. Leona told me that when her body enters the frigid water, she actually experiences a form of paralysis. After getting out of the water, drying off, getting dressed and thawing out, she transforms this initial sensation into feeling like it is time to move toward her goals and desires. Leona was initially fearful of participating in this event. The biggest accomplishment was getting over that fear. She had to trust the process of jumping into the lake and surviving.

In business, it is the same. We need to jump in and abolish fear. Fear is the one thing that does hold us back or paralyzes us from reaching our goals.

We all need the desire to grow, yet some people are lacking this motivation and stop growing and learning. No matter how young or old you are, learning will inspire growth. Maybe you are in the midst of a challenging growth period and you are looking for insight and direction or maybe you are in search of tools to help you grow. When I reflect over the past few years, I realize that there was a point where I had stopped growing. I was so backed into my shell and didn't even realize it. I ventured on a path of learning in search of the growth that had ceased. The opportunities that I was presented with were plentiful. With desire comes passion and with passion comes success.

With desire comes passion and with passion comes success.

In sales we need the passion to go out and make the next sale. We need the passion to make our call list and then get on the phone to make the calls. We need the passion to be real so that it shines through when we make the introductory call and our customers want it. We need passion to ask for the sale and the same passion when we deliver or complete the transaction. If your goals are a passion, they will happen!

My New Year's resolution this year was to grow and improve my skills. I appreciate how far I have come and I will continue to strive to go further. Only I have control over my performance. Do I want it to be mediocre or fantastic?

Recently I had the opportunity to have lunch with some friends. They run a very successful business and work with entrepreneurs all over the world. In their office there is a big banner that reads:

"Make your future greater than your past."

That day when I walked into their office, I stopped and looked at that banner. In this profound moment, I realized that sometimes we just stroll along without striving to make our future greater than our past. We don't invest in ourselves for the betterment of our future or for others.

Make your future greater than your past.

The only person that can have control over your performance is you. So I invite you to jump into the "now" with me — perhaps not into Lake Ontario but with renewed mind for growth. Be willing to learn. Be willing to embrace your fears. This jump only requires a shift in your mindset and attitude. You must first make this jump in your mind and then with your actions through determination.

What kind of action and hustle needs to happen to increase your sales? Can I challenge you to step out of the box this month and go for it?

You will always feel fear; I think we all will in some form or another. If we allow trust to be bigger than fear we will create more business than we can handle. All of a sudden our phones will be ringing for appointments and sales will be made. You will find a $20 bill in your coat pocket and have no trouble paying the bills. People will be calling you for business, not you calling them for business. Your victories will come more quickly!

What are you willing to commit to your life and business? Keep learning and stay teachable! Be a willing student. Your family deserves it and so do you.

What constantly surprises me is the answer I get when I ask people what it is they REALLY want. Most don't have an answer. Sure, they may have one or two big goals for themselves, but they have never really taken the time to decide what they want from every area of their life. Why not take half an hour to sit quietly by yourself right now, yes right now, and ask yourself that question. "What do I really want from my life and business?" The choice is yours to make. No one can ever care more about your success than you do.

Go for it!

Chapter 4

An Ant's Determination

There are people who make things happen;
Who watch things happen;
Who ask what happened...
Which one are you?

I was gardening the other day and as I sat on the grass there was a mound of ants to my side. There were so many in a pile that I stopped what I was doing to observe their movements. It was such an interesting sight that I sat there staring for a long time and this is what I observed.

Ants never quit! What a great philosophy. If they were headed somewhere and I tried to stop them, they looked for another way to get around me, over me or under me. They were persistent and kept looking for another free path to travel. They were determined. Now, apply this philosophy to sales; never quit searching for where you are supposed to go.

It was October and the ants were collecting food in preparation for winter. They were planning ahead. That is another important perspective. They were all so busy, carrying heavy loads. I wondered how they knew when they had enough food, but watching them, they just kept going after more, never stopping. In sales, when we have enough, we stop. Why do we do that? If we have a great week selling, we stop on Friday at noon! Why don't we keep on going like there is no end? The ants were gathering all they possibly could. Why don't we do all we possibly can? Summer tends to slow us down and we don't prepare well enough for the busy winter in sales. We can't be so naïve. We need to gather business in the summer just as efficiently as we do in the winter so we don't starve. It is important to think ahead and plan. If we relax too much, we may be unprepared for the potential storm ahead.

History is filled with people who were advised to quit just short of great accomplishments. Benjamin Franklin was told by experts to leave alone all that foolish experimenting with lightning. They said it was a waste of time. Fortunately he did not quit, he was determined.

Henry Ford was urged by Thomas Edison to abandon his work on the idea of a motor car. "It is a worthless idea," remarked Edison. Henry Ford would not quit, he was determined.

Orville and Wilbur Wright were spending a lot of time and energy on something that would fly into the air. In 1908 on a field in Kitty Hawk, NC, the brothers taxied their idea down a homemade runway and launched us into the era of flight. Orville and Wilbur would not quit, they were determined.

Abraham Lincoln ran for legislature and failed. He entered business and failed, spending 17 years paying off his debts. He ran for congress and was not elected. He ran for the United States Senate and lost. He finally became President of the United States. Abraham Lincoln would not quit, he was determined.

Thomas Edison went through over 1,000 experiments before discovering the light bulb. Thomas Edison would not quit, he was determined.

Christopher Columbus had to face a panel of experts headed by Spain's leading geographer who examined his plans and presented the findings to the King and Queen of Portugal. They wrote, "Columbus' plan cannot be accomplished. Quite impossible." Christopher Columbus did not quit, he was determined.

The key that unlocks the door to success is determination. Without a key, the door will never open. Most frustrated quitters never achieve their potential, not because of challenges, but because of the failure to be determined, persistent and commit to their goals, dreams and desires. The level of your determination to accomplish your goals is measured by what it takes to make you quit.

> **The level of your determination to accomplish your goals is measured by what it takes to make you quit.**

There is one common link between the successes and failures I have had. ME.

I am responsible for my health, for my attitude, for the income I bring in, for the relationships I have with my family and friends and for how I act on a daily basis. Whether things are going well or not, I always have to look at what I am doing and debrief. What is working? What is not working? What am I learning from the situation? When things are going well I need to celebrate the win and when things aren't going well I need to re-evaluate what I am doing. I can't blame anyone if my business isn't going the way I want it to. Working in direct sales, I have heard people say things like, "I didn't get any help from my leader, that is why I am quitting," as an example. Did that person come to the meetings, read the newsletter or get on the conference call? Or better yet, did they even ask for help? It is time to stop blaming other people for your lack of success. When you blame others, it will just kill your energy. If you are around people who are negative, stop hanging out with them, they will deplete your energy too. We need to realize that we do have a choice... we can stay where we are or we can take responsibility and do something different. Change isn't easy but it is necessary to move ahead.

As we learned from the amazing people mentioned above, we need to take responsibility and believe in ourselves. We have to be willing to take the risks necessary to get where we want to be. It is great to know that our success really does depend on ourselves. If we are determined, we can have whatever we want.

Be like the ant. Decide to make changes one step at a time. You may have to go over, under or through an obstacle, but once you start the process you will find out that it is much easier to get what you want by taking control of your own destiny.

Chapter 5

What Does it Mean to be Relentless?

Have you ever woken up with an intense sense of clarity? One morning I woke up before my alarm clock sounded and I felt an intense sense of purpose. I had been very busy with business and quite frankly felt like I was in overwhelm mode. Have you ever felt like that? Maybe you are there right now?

When I went for my morning run, I couldn't stop thinking about what my purpose is here on earth. I came to the conclusion that my purpose is to make a difference in the world. What is your purpose? Why are you here? What drives you? For me, it is about being relentless. Doing what nobody else will do. It is about changing the world one sale at a time. It is about building relationships and building a foundation for my life and business.

I am on this planet to WIN. I hate losing. When I see people not challenging themselves to reach their potential it burns me up inside. When I feel stagnant, the panic button goes off loud and clear. I want to make a difference. I want to be relentless to the point that nothing can hold me back or stop me. I don't want to be denied success or reaching my dreams. Why is it that we hit points in our lives like this, where we go full tilt and give our business everything we have? And then there are other days where we don't put an ounce of effort into it? We lie down and let life roll us over.

Every week I step out onto the volleyball court with one desire in mind and that is to win. Why even step on the court if your desire isn't to win? You don't walk out on the court to lose. Winning is addictive. I get up in the morning ready to win. Is your desire to win? I hang out with people who want to win and challenge themselves to go for it. There have been times in my business when I have come second in a contest. What that means to me at this time is that I am the first loser. Losing isn't bad; it just depends on how you take losing? Does it push you to drive harder or does it make you give up?

At what point do you feel relentless, where you can't be stopped? Where do you draw your line in the sand? When will you stop kidding yourself and release your potential to the world? Are you playing not to lose? This is different from playing to win! When will you refuse to give up another inch?

I'd like to share with you an excerpt from the movie *Boiler Room*. Here, a pep-talk is being given to sales staff by the supervisor: "And there's no such thing as a 'no sale' call. A sale is made on every call you make. Either you sell the client some stock or he sells you on a reason he can't. Either way a sale is made. The only question is who's going to close? You or him? Now be relentless! That's it! I'm done!"

That says it all. On a previous trip I took with my husband and our friends to Nassau, Bahamas, we were standing by the marina in front of Atlantis. We saw a 130' yacht that was breathtaking. The name on the back of the yacht was *RELENTLESS*. Another 150' yacht was named *IMAGINE*. In order for the yacht owners to have their 130' yachts, they had to go after their dreams, passions and desires.

What is your mission in life? What are you relentless about? Can you vividly imagine your dreams coming true?

Chapter 6

Create a Visual Picture

At the beginning of each New Year I create a new goal board. A goal board is a collage of pictures and words that I cut and paste onto a piece of bristol board. When complete, I hang it in my office and review it at the end of each month. The board helps me to see where I am going and what I have accomplished. It is a visual affirmation for each goal I have set. Once my board is made, I expect results from myself.

At the end of the year, I look back and visually see how many goals I have made come true. This is a time to celebrate the victories and re-evaluate the goals that didn't happen. Are they still important, do I need to change them or what do I need to do to make them happen in the following year?

Celebrate victories and re-evaluate goals that did not happen.

I started doing a vision board 15 years ago. There was a company contest where you could win a trip to New York City plus $500 spending money. I really wanted this trip, so I told my family about my plan. That night I was at work and when I came home my daughter had created a vision board for me. She was seven years old at the time. It was bright, lime green and she had put the numbers 1-54 around the outside of the board and a big 55 in the middle. To win this contest I needed 55 points. She got the company magazine that had the contest details in it and cut and pasted all the fun things that we would do in NYC. When I saw the vision board it brought tears to my eyes because my daughter knew just how much I wanted to win the trip and she was going to help me get there. I had no choice but to win the contest. Every time I got a point she would run to my office and cross off the points. As I got closer and closer, the pressure rose but I was determined. When the last point was earned I remember her jumping up and down telling me that I was a winner. I will never forget that moment and how good it felt to accomplish a goal I had been determined to reach.

From that moment on I have had a vision board in my office and it has helped me reach goals that I never thought I could.

If you have never done this before, it's easy. All you need is a pair of scissors, a glue stick and some magazines. Cut out anything that speaks to you whether it is a word, phrase or photo. For instance, if you want to lose weight, put a photo of someone exercising or eating a salad on your board. If you want a new car, put a photo of the exact car you want on your board. If you want to increase sales, put the exact amount you want to increase by. As you reach the goals, circle them at the end of each month. You don't even need to go out and buy magazines. Go to your local library and they should sell old magazines for anywhere from 10 cents to 25 cents each.

You will be amazed at yourself and your abilities. Have a clear vision for your future.

My Vision Board for 2008

Chapter 7

How to Anchor Your Victories

Blair Singer, one of Robert Kiyosaki's Rich Dad's Advisors, says, "Sales is an emotional contact sport — highest energy wins." When your emotion is down, we simply lose our energy. The key is to find a way to generate energy when we need it the most.

> "Sales is an emotional contact sport — highest energy wins."

Think of a time when you were really successful and anchor that moment in your mind. It is vital to be able to store, or anchor, this moment and recall it when needed. It's a simple process. Take your hand and put it into a fist. If you have ever seen the movie Home Alone, every time Kevin (Macaulay Culkin) pulled one over on the bad guys he said, "yes!", while he made a fist and pumped his arm in towards his core. So on the count of three, think about your success, pull it in and anchor. Ready, one… two… three… YES! Since learning is a process, before I go on any sales call I anchor my success. When I get a win, I anchor my new success.

When someone says no, I anchor the success of being closer to a win. Did you know that no doesn't really mean no in my mind. It means, not now. Take it a step further. When you get an appointment with a client, anchor that success. When you have the initial meeting with your prospect, anchor that success. When you are asked for a proposal, anchor that success. When you have a meeting to go over the proposal, anchor that success. When you get the order, anchor that success. When you deliver the order, anchor that success. When you get a testimonial, anchor that success. When you get a referral, anchor that success. Your energy will go up and so will your results — remember, the highest energy wins!

I was at a local office supply store recently purchasing some business supplies. As I was walking down the aisle I noticed an "EASY" button. You've probably seen it on TV. I couldn't help but to press it. Instantly I smiled so I pressed it again and laughed. I couldn't resist putting it into my cart. It cost around $6.00 and well worth every cent, I have had so much fun with it. I had my sales team go out and purchase the "Easy" button. At every training session someone gets to press it and instantly our energy is raised. When I get my book work done, I press it. When I make a sale, I press it and anchor my success. When we really look at sales we can say "that was easy."

Chapter 8

Go Red

In society today, green means go, yellow means caution and red means stop. Flashing red lights get our attention.

If we turn this theory around in sales and make Red equal to Go, can you imagine the possibilities? Red is my personal favorite color. When I wear it in sales it gives me more energy, creates passion and excitement. When my energy is low, I put on a red suit and my attitude changes. Red is a strong, hot color and it has been proven that red can have physical effects including raising blood pressure.

I was speaking with a girlfriend the other day who was having a tough time with her business which made her very angry. When telling me about a particular situation she said, "I was so mad that I saw red." At that moment her face got red and her physical stature changed. When we face frustration in business this can happen.

In the business world, red represents power. When you see a salesman wearing a red tie, it gives him more power. Watching the Emmy awards, the stars all walk down the red carpet, which is rolled out for very important people. Each year I roll out a red carpet at my annual sales awards for my sales people and they love it.

When I was picking up Chinese food one night I asked why they chose to use the color red in their restaurant. The owner told me that in China, red is the color of prosperity and happiness, and brings good luck.

In sales, red makes me take action to get into gear. It makes me speed forward and gives me more confidence.

Red can also be a sign of being tired. My daughter recently took the red eye flight home from Las Vegas and her eyes were so red they showed how tired she was. When we get this way in business we need to get rest and know that it is okay to refuel ourselves.

From now on, as you drive down the road and see the red lights that usually aggravate us, change your mindset and think of all the passion they could bring to your business. Let red move you forward. Go buy yourself that fantastic red suit or tie and see how you feel when you put it on. Track your results in sales as you wear this bright, cheerful color.

What gear are you in right now? Are you moving with caution, moving ahead or stopped? As entrepreneurs, business owners or employees, we must always keep in motion. When we take our foot off the brake, we can move forward to speed up our success when our intentions are set right.

Chapter 9

Results Rather Than Status

A new business partner and I were having a discussion about our businesses. We got talking about my career and I was telling him of my successes with my Direct Sales business. I have been in the Direct Sales industry for 20 years and have been the top in sales numerous times, the top in Leadership and have won more things than you can imagine. Some of my winnings include trips all over the world, seven fur coats, furniture, designer suits, office equipment,... The rewards and recognition of accomplishment bring personal satisfaction, but we have to remember their true intention.

A few years ago I had some personal troubles, my mom had a heart attack, my brother-in-law Bill passed away from cancer and my husband and sister's partnership dissolved after working together for 10 years. The air in my balloon had been deflated to say the least. It was around this time that we were having our yearly seminar for my Direct Sales business. With these distractions, my sales were down and I was winning lower level achievement prizes. Up to that time I had always won the top prizes.

I was feeling bad about my performance but what got in the way more than that was what I thought other people were going to think. Before the seminar I decided to put in an extra order to bring my volume up so I would earn the next level prize. The order I put in brought me up to reach the "$8,000 Personal Best" prize level. I remember going up on stage to receive my award certificate and not feeling right about the whole thing. When I got home and unpacked my personal best prize I sat there stunned! I call it my $8,000 paper shredder because that is the "personal best" prize I won, or should I honestly say, bought into. For a very long time, every time I looked at that paper shredder in my office, I felt like kicking it. To this day I have never shredded a single piece of paper in it and have put it in my husband's office to remove it from my sight. When I shared this story with a colleague, he laughed so hard. He said, you should have the paper shredder mounted and have a plaque put on the mount that says, "How not to let your ego get in the way of sales." We both laughed.

This was a very big learning lesson for me throughout the years. That paper shredder has taught me more than you would have expected. First, it taught me to take time for myself when I need a time out. Life isn't always peaches and cream and when situations arise, we need to acknowledge what is going on. We don't need to prove anything to anyone else. I often wonder if anyone in the entire company remembers me even earning that paper shredder. The answer is 99% no! The 1% who remembers me walking up on the stage to accept my award is ME.

I was recently reading a book called the *The Laws of Lifetime Growth* by Dan Sullivan. In the book, Dan has a section about being honest about your motives. He says: "Why are you really doing what you are doing? Is it about you and your own advancement or is it about creating a result that will benefit others? Which are you more committed to? What does your behavior say? Sometimes we can surprise ourselves with the answers to those questions. If your ego or your need for status is getting in the way of creating the best results for others, be aware that this leaves you standing still, just waiting to be bypassed by someone who is fully committed just to getting the result. Rather than trying to defend yourself against this kind of bypass, it's much more rewarding to stop undermining your growth with status seeking and take on a more cooperative attitude." True wisdom about success!

"Why are you really doing what you are doing?

For me, the paper shredder symbolized the need for status. I worried about what others would think rather than achieving what I had wanted.

Once I got myself back on my feet and got back to my mission of helping others succeed in business, the rewards followed. In my business the reward has always come back 10-fold when I placed my energy on results rather than status.

Learn from the lessons of your life and celebrate! Again, never stop learning and growing and put your ego in check. Strive for results, not status.

Chapter 10

Momentum

Back in the early 1800s there were these two old men standing out in the edge of a field watching a team of men working feverishly on one of the first steam locomotives.

It was a massive beast of a machine unlike anything they had ever seen before. As the team put the finishing touches on the giant locomotive, the first man asked, "What do you think?" Then the second man turned and replied bluntly, "They'll never get that big thing going."

The two old men watched curiously as the team stoked the fires and the engine spewed steam from its smoke stack. More and more steam poured from the stack and then all of a sudden the wheels began to move.

At first the wheels would just slip and then grab as it slowly inched its way along. Finally it caught traction and started off down the track. Five miles per hour, then ten, then fifteen, then twenty miles per hour — roaring down the track.

The first old man turned back to the other and asked, "Well, what do you think now?" Then the second man turned and replied calmly, "They'll never get that big thing stopped.

This is the way sales work. It takes effort to get it going, but once you do, you'll never get stopped. Sometimes we ask the "what do you think" question to our peers or family. Sometimes the worst advice is free advice. If I had listened to my friends and family when they told me that quitting my full time job to go into business for myself was crazy, I would not have started my business. Now, like the train story, they all tell me how wonderful it is that I left my job because of the success I've gained.

Sometimes the worst advice is free.

This past summer when I was stepping onto our boat from the dock, a thought came to my mind. Once you put your foot forward onto the boat, you relinquish your former position. Once momentum has started you can continue to go forward or exert energy to make you step backwards. If you stop mid stream, you will fall into the water.

Sometimes in business we get root bound. I was attempting to transplant a large plant, and when I got it out of the pot, the roots were all tangled together and woven very tight. It was impossible to separate them, so I had to cut through the roots to split the plant up. A few weeks later, life started to come back into the three individual sections of the plant I had divided up. Their roots had had time to grow and room to spread out. When we have been doing the same old thing in business it is easy to see why we get root bound. What can you do to transplant yourself in your business? What can you do to create momentum and growth? Are you ready to expand or are you stuck in the same old pot and can't breathe? What action do you need to take to play a bigger game?

According to the late and great Earl Nightingale, success is directly proportional to three things:

1. The need for what you do
2. Your ability to do it
3. The difficulty of replacing you

Robert Kiyosaki said, “defeat fear by gaining knowledge and confidence.”

And Eleanor Roosevelt said, "yesterday is history, tomorrow is a mystery, and today is a gift; that's why they call it the present."

Stick with your plan and desires and see them through to completion. I saw a little boy the other day chasing two rabbits out of the garden. They both hopped in the same direction until he started to chase them. Once the chase was on, the rabbits went in different directions. The boy ran back and forth until he lost sight of both rabbits. I have seen this happen in business when people have divided focus and are chasing too many things. In the end we don't catch anything or close any business. Keep on the right track.

Momentum is gaining the desired result by repeating successful actions

Momentum is gaining the desired result by repeating successful actions — once in motion the results tend to keep coming and like the train, we start to head in the desired direction.

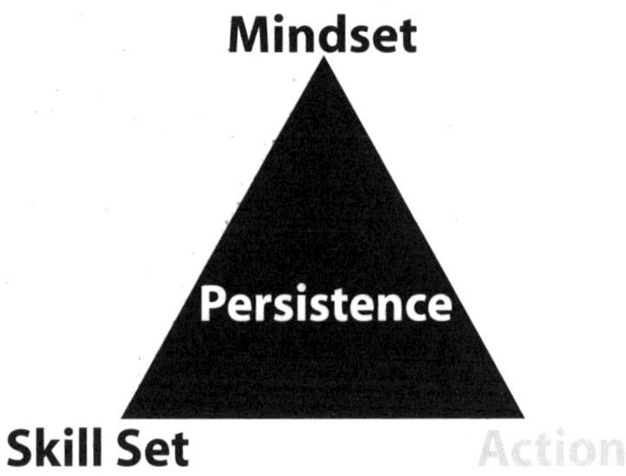
Mindset
Persistence
Skill Set
Action

PART 2
Skill Set

Chapter 11

Skill Set Introduction

"There is no short cut to achievement.
Life requires thorough preparation —
veneer isn't worth anything."
George Washington Carver

Everything can be learned, all you have to do is take ownership of your skills. I was watching my great niece, Kate, learning how to walk. She took great energy in pulling herself up onto the couch only to take one step and tumble to the ground. She made attempt after attempt until she started to cry when she fell too hard. We sat on the couch and encouraged her with a clap when she took a step. It is always amazing watching a baby take their first steps. At first, the child does not have the skill set to walk. They have to be persistent, keep trying even though they fall, get bumped and banged and discouraged. But, they don't give up. To them it is a great challenge. It is amazing how quickly they go from stumbling to running.

When you start a new job or business, you have to learn the skill set. My first job was at a Greek Restaurant as a dishwasher. It paid $2.00 an hour, under the table, because I was only 14 years old. In between dish loads I would spend time with the cook watching what he was doing and, in no time, I was helping him prepare shrimp cocktails and entrees. It was a good learning experience for me and to this day I make a mean shrimp cocktail and can fit more than average into my dishwasher. That skill set stayed with me.

I have been self employed for 20 years, so learning how to run a successful business was very important to me. I realized that I had to invest in my own learning. I have taken courses from great leaders and implemented what I learned into my business. Some of the leaders I have learned from are: Blair Singer, Robert Kiyosaki, T. Harv Ecker, Darren Weeks, Bob Proctor, Zig Zigler, Anthony Robbins, and Dan Sullivan, to name a few. The investment of money to attend was a business write off and I have made the money back many times over. I have met many people who run from seminar to seminar and don't implement their learning. To me, that is a waste of both time and money. People get high on the seminars but don't take the skills they have learned to move ahead. Go, learn and take the skills to improve your business. To have success, I believe that you have to be constantly learning and improving your skills to stay ahead of the pack. The best part, though, is teaching what you learn. Even if you don't have a team, when you learn something new, teach a friend, neighbor or child. When you can teach something, you have really learned it well. Own the skill!

Take the skills you've learned and move ahead

Chapter 12

The 15 Most Critical Words in Your Sales Vocabulary

...and how to use them

Activity: In business, if we are not active we are standing still. Without activity in business, there are no sales. Without sales, there is no income. The word active also means to keep your body active. 30 minutes of exercise every day will achieve this and give you more energy for your business and your family. We must also keep our mind active by filling it with positive thoughts and information. Read an inspirational book and keep learning. Why not read more books this year than you did last year? Listen to motivational audios in your car. This positive influence will help you become more active and give you great ideas.

Chance: What if today you could take a chance? You know, do something you have never done before. Why is it that we hold back on taking chances? Is it the risk of failure? Recently, I was skiing in Fernie, British Columbia. There was powder snow up to my knees on the un-groomed trails and less snow on the groomed hills. I decided to take a chance and ski through the powder. You know what happened? I had fun!! I also fell, but got up, dusted myself off and moved on. If I never took the chance I would have never known what it would have felt like to ski through powder. In business, we can take the easy route or take a chance with a more challenging one. If we are going to make a mistake, we must make it quickly, learn from it and move on. What chance can you take in your business to create opportunity for yourself and your career? You might fall and have to dust yourself off, but let me tell you, it is a rush and will be worth it. Do the "one thing" you have always wanted to do. You will never know how much power you have until you take on something risky and take a chance. Power is the ability to create, hold and change position.

Determination: What do you want to accomplish? Are you determined to reach your target? We all need to have determination in us. An example of this came when I was training a company. I had sent them out to make introductory calls and it was a contest to see who could bring back the most business cards. One of the plant employees Mark, whose car was in getting serviced, had never made a sales call in his life. Most people would have made excuses as to why they couldn't participate, like not having a car. However, he was determined to take part in this contest so off he went, on foot, to make calls. In the end, his determination landed him 19 business cards and first place.

Discipline: What are you willing to do to discipline yourself to get out there and make another sale? What strength do you have to reach your goal? In the same training as above, one of the participants tried to make a cold call one year ago and could not do it. His fear took over and he gave up. When he was challenged to go out and do it this time, he conquered his fear and was disciplined to not only make one call but he continued on to make two calls. He was so pumped when he got back. Be disciplined on planning your day…what outcome do you want?

Denial: When we aren't selling enough and don't want to look at our stats, we go into denial mode. Instead of just acknowledging what state your business is in and doing something about it, it is sometimes easier to go into this mode and tell everyone that our business is doing great. Then we stop our workday early, sleep in, think of a million things to do other than what we should be doing. During another cold calling game, one participant said she made the calls but when it came to sharing their experiences with the group she confessed that she really didn't make any. Fear took over her. As a group, we were proud of her honesty, however, I warned her that she may have to get back out there next week. Denial can take over if we let it. Think about your business....what puts you into denial mode?

Focus: Robert Kiyosaki describes this perfectly by giving each letter a great meaning. F-follow, O-one, C-course, U-until, S-successful. Sometimes we have our eye on so many things that we don't accomplish anything. Think about going to the gym. The first few weeks after we start working out we are totally focused, but what happens as time goes on? Why do we become unfocused? In business, we are focused when everything is going well, however this changes when things start heading south. What course are you following both personally and in your business? Have a positive focus every day. List three things at the end of the day that you achieved. This positive focus will re-enforce your wins and increase your energy.

F - ollow
O - ne
C - ourse
U - ntil
S - uccessful

Money: During our sales conference calls, every time someone says "money" everyone does a cheer. Why do we do this? To celebrate the win! Money means a sale has been made. Do you want to increase your income this week, month, year? Do you have a game plan on how you can do this? Set the dollar amount that you would like to increase it by and then chart out the way to do it. Maybe it is one more sale, one more cold call or one more new client each day. Decide what it is that will give you an increase and set the intention to make it happen for you. We all need money to survive and money can give us the lifestyle we want. What lifestyle do you want and how much money will it take per month for you to have what you want?

Drive: Is your tank full or empty? Are you using regular gas or premium? Are you on cruise control? Have you lost direction? Every journey that we take in business needs to have a clear destination. What is your vision for the road ahead? We need to fuel our bodies so that we can drive our business. What drives you in life? What keeps you going strong? Are you driving fast or slow? Are you hanging around people who are moving faster than you are or slower? Are you driving a team? Each person on the team might have a different destination but they may have all the same tools. Sometimes those who are moving slower can hold us back yet those who are moving full steam ahead can motivate us to do better, to want more for ourselves and our families. What drives you to keep on going? In order to get what you want, you must first decide what you want. Many people don't know what they want or can't see how it would be possible to get what they want. Maybe the drive isn't great enough to allow them to get what they want. Are you ready to get started? You can do it. Switch your drive into forward and go for it. Tell others what you want and when you want it by.

Thought: A thought turns into action and an action turns into a sale. When you get a thought, simply take action and you will see results. We can have the best ideas when we are sleeping. We wake up and think, "Wow what a great idea," only to get up in the morning and forget what that thought was about. Have a note pad and a pen beside your bed and when you wake up in the middle of the night with that great idea, write it down so in the morning you can take action on it. In the car have a voice recorder to capture that thought that comes to your mind so you can act on it when you get to the office or home. Some modern cell phones have a voice recorder and can help you with this.

Results: After you have the thought and take action, the next step will be the result. If the results are not what you want, then you may need to practice your presentation and technique. You need to seriously take a look at what actions you are taking and change what you are doing. When you are polished you will become more confident and congruent. When you take action with confidence you will see positive results. When you wake up in the morning complete the

following statement:
My purpose today is to________________. Anchor the result you want each day.

De-Clutter: Start today by clearing up the clutter in your home, your office, your car. A messy car reflects on you if it is dirty and there is garbage lying around on the inside. A clean car is so important for your image. Get the pile of paperwork off your desk and floor. Clear the space by your phone so you can get to the receiver. Go in your closet and get rid of all the clothes you don't wear and those that don't fit. Clean out your kitchen cupboards and especially your junk drawer. By clearing your office space and your living space you will have more room to grow. A friend of mine, Kim, told me if I hadn't touched it in six months, I should remove it from my office and that it was taking up valuable space. It was great advice.

Appreciation: Do you appreciate every sale you make? Do you appreciate your customers? Do you treat the customer who buys a small ticket item just like the customer who buys your most expensive product? Do you appreciate your business or your employees? Do you appreciate yourself and what you have accomplished? Do you appreciate your skills? Do you appreciate those around you that ask more of you than you ask of yourself? Practice gratitude. It is the ultimate anti-depressant. Engage in daily random acts of kindness. Appreciate the smiles you receive and the smiles you give away. This week, take time to tell five people that you really appreciate them. You can do this in person, on the phone or send them a note in the mail.

> **Give yourself permission to go for it!**

Dream: Dream it, believe it and achieve it! Let yourself dream and dream big. Go after your dream and you will come up with ideas on how you can attain your dream. People will start showing up to help you get there and opportunities will arise. Don't hold yourself back from your dreams, think big and play big and all your dreams and desires will come true. Dream beyond what you thought you could. Set a course of action to get there. Give yourself permission to go for it. Hang around with others who will inspire your dreams to come true. Dream about who you want to become, what legacy you want to leave behind…dream big and go for it! Dream big enough that it scares you… really stretch yourself. Why not dream with energy and enthusiasm. Dream while you are awake, not asleep!

Serve: Why is it important to serve first? As a recipient of The Citizen of the Year Award in my community, service has always been at the top of my list. When I serve, business comes back to me in leaps and bounds. Helping others get what they want will only help you get what you want. When your dreams include serving and helping others, they will come true. People want to help people and when you see the difference it makes in the lives you touch by serving it makes all the difference in the world. Using your energy in a positive way will be of service not only to yourself but to your business. Don't waste your energy by having negative thoughts. Hang out with positive people and be positive in the moment.

Goals: Write your goals down in detail and post them somewhere you can see them every day. Refer to your list so you know where you are and when you meet a goal, highlight it and create a new goal. Goals must be measurable. Keep your goals wide-ranging and have goals for different areas in your life such as your health, your finances, your career, your family and your relationships. Look to the future and ask yourself, “What do I want to accomplish three years from now?”

Chapter 13

Learn From Your Mistakes

My husband and I have won in business ventures and lost in business ventures. We have made a lot of money and lost money. Throughout our journey there has always been a lesson to be learned in every situation. The question is, can you acknowledge the lesson? After you acknowledge the lesson, can you learn from it? Or do you let it take you out? There is no such thing as a failure if you acknowledge the lesson!

There is no such thing as a failure if you acknowledge the lesson!

Our first business venture was when we were newly married. We just celebrated our 25 year anniversary — YES! (Remember, celebrate all victories!) We sold door alarm screamers through the TV Guide. They bolted straight on to your door and let out a scream when it opened. When we were setting up the business we didn't ask anyone for their advice except the company that helped us get started. We didn't want to have any negative comments coming from friends or family so we never told anyone until we got our first order from TV Guide, after which we told everyone. That was the only order we ever got. We had to buy 150 of them to start off, too! We tried everything to sell those door alarms. We went to flee markets and craft shows. It got to be so funny because for about five years, everyone in our family got one for Christmas. The trick was to package them differently so I surprised them every year. We had some fun with those screamers. Eventually we just got rid of them so that negative energy wasn't around us anymore. The lesson there was that we didn't do our market research before we jumped in. We bought the first product that was pitched to us due to our excitement of getting into business. We did not do our due diligence.

We invested in another company five years ago. The concept of the business was incredible and our excitement for this concept moved us to buy not one share at $15,000 but two shares. It didn't take long for the business to start going down hill. It was mismanaged and the owner took it to bankruptcy. Here we had invested $30,000 of our savings and it was now all gone and there was no way we were going to recoup our losses. The feelings of disappointment, frustration, anger, mistrust, hurt, worry and fear were overwhelming. We were sick to our stomachs and couldn't stop thinking about what we were going to do next. Not only did we invest $30,000, but the owner asked us to lend him $5,000 for a short period of time. Guess what? We never saw that money again either. I don't think I will ever totally understand how people can take advantage of others and feel good about themselves when they borrow money and don't repay it. But that is for them to live with, not those who are taken advantage of.

How do you deal with this? Well, it takes some time but letting it go and forgiving the situation is the best recipe. You can hold it in and let it eat you up inside or you can release the stress and figure out a way to move forward. People lose money in business all the time. We are not the first and we won't be the last but we are very aware now. We don't jump into opportunities anymore without checking things out very carefully. We don't buy on excitement, we buy on stats.

The above business was replicated and it is very successful today.

The lesson was to keep track of the metrics or statistics. Keep track of who you have invested with. Do they have a good track record? Are they reliable? It turned out that the person we invested in was a personal acquaintance who was terrible at managing the money and was not reliable. Funny thing is that I knew this before we invested but we loved the idea so much we invested anyway. That inner voice inside our head that screams at us to not do something is right every time. Listen to those gut feelings in the pit of your stomach. My husband and I also learned to go with our instincts. If it doesn't feel right it probably isn't right.

Did we survive our failed business ventures? Absolutely. Did we learn from them? Yes. I don't regret either venture because it just helped us in so many other areas of life and business.

Learn from the failures in your life and celebrate! Learn from your mistakes. Don't give up. Again, never stop learning and growing.

> **Learn from the mistakes in your life and celebrate!**

This theory applies also to Sales. We don't always get the sale and sometimes we want to give up. You are going to think I have totally lost it here, but I challenge you to play the "NO GAME." When my stats aren't where they need to be, I play this game myself. I see how many no's I can get in a single day, week, or month. By the time I start tracking my no's, I end up getting more yeses. Before I know it, I am back on track. You see, when we are hit with no's we stop trying as hard and get discouraged. If you play the NO GAME, you will have fun and see your results turn around.

The key to adversity is to always be learning and growing personally. When I am driving in my car, I never have the radio on during business hours. I always listen to motivational and instructional CDs. This keeps my brain active and I am learning every day. I also read great books that give me ideas and challenges. I go to seminars. Yes they cost money to attend, but the value that I get back is worth so much more. Hang out with successful business owners and ask them how they made it. What did they do to get to their level of success? And the greatest tip I can give you is to have a mentor, someone who you are accountable to and someone who will inspire you to be the best that you can be and push you outside of your comfort zone. This is an investment in you, not an expense, as many people see it.

Chapter 14

Learn To Motivate Yourself

Stop Making Excuses!

I hear more excuses in business than you can imagine. When a client starts handing me the Excuse Bag, it is my job to tell them the truth. That is a job that isn't always easy, but necessary. If you want to reach your goals, remember the importance of energy. If you put two people together in a selling situation, the one with the highest energy will win and get the sale. Concentrate your energy on what is working rather than what isn't working. If something didn't work, learn from it and move on. A friend of mine has been telling me for about a year that she wants to go to the gym. I asked her this week what is holding her back. She said she didn't have the money right now to go and buy workout clothes. I told her to exercise in a pair of shorts and a tee shirt, who cares if you don't have that matching designer outfit! Let's face it, excuses creep up on our lives all the time. Focus your energy on what works and excuses will go away.

Principles to Live By

What principles do you live your life by? If you are not accountable to yourself, then who can you be accountable to? Some of the principles that I live by (in no particular order) are:

- Expect more from myself than others do.
- Maintain continual spiritual growth and personal development.

- Eat healthy and look after my body by exercising.
- Have fun.
- Give back to the community and those in need.
- Make my future bigger than my past.
- Quality family time.

Do I have to call on myself for the principles that I set? Yes, and then I get back on track. Our family has a set of principles to live by, too. I remember the day we sat at the kitchen table and discussed the principles that we wanted our family to live by. Our son Kyle, who was 19, said, “To have lots of fun”, which was a great item to have on the list. Megan, who was 21, wanted to support each other no matter what. My husband and I put down to never go to bed mad at each other. Do we need to call on each other when our principles are not followed? Yes. The good thing is that “calling” is part of the process — once you have agreed to the principles, anyone involved can “call” you on it when you don't follow them. In this case, our children can call us if we don't follow the family's principles. Since creating the code, we don't seem to have blow ups. It gets handled sooner and with less stress. We are all accountable to each other. We need to let the kids know where we are just as much as they need to let us know where they are.

In business, principles to work by are imperative and that is the first thing we work on when we help out companies. We have seen tremendous results from simply putting principles into place. The business owners and employees work together harmoniously in the workplace.

Model Success

A great way to increase your business is to model your behavior after a successful achiever, someone you admire or want to get to know. Take this person out to lunch and ask them how they became successful. They will be more than happy to share their story with you. Remember, if you always do what you have always done, you always get what you have always gotten. Find out how others do it.

Be open to improvement — remember the importance of being a willing student.

If you always do what you have always done, you always get what you have always gotten.

After being in the direct selling industry for 20 years, I was giving a talk to my sales team. I asked them three questions:

1. Do you believe in our product?
2. Would you buy the product if you were not in this business?
3. Are you enthused about sales — the profession you are in?

People want to do business with like-minded people. They want to deal with people who know what they are talking about, someone who is an expert in their field. They also want to trust, like and enjoy listening to you. Are you polished? Have you practiced your presentation?

When a sale is not made, it can be explained by one of three reasons:

1. They are not ready to buy or don't have a need for the product.
2. They can't afford the product at the moment.
3. They don't like you or your presentation.

If you don't mesh with your customer, don't put yourself down. Find someone else to talk to. Here is a fact that you might be interested in. As of the date of this entry:

According to the International Programs Center, U.S. Census Bureau, the total population of the World, projected to 02/28/08 at 15:31 GMT (EST+5) is:

6,653,494,098

There are lots of customers out there in the world. If someone doesn't want to buy, find someone else to talk to. If you talk to enough people you will sell. You will find people who need your product and that it is the right time to buy. You will find people who you connect with and will want to buy from you.

I was clearing out my filing cabinet and came across some very large files that contained the names of all the people I have brought into my business over the past 20 years. As I skimmed through the folders I was actually amazed at how many of those people are no longer in my business. At first this made me feel uncomfortable, but the more I thought about it, I came to realize that a lot of people don't want to be doing what I am doing. Some try it and it just isn't for them and some have tried it and have had long, successful businesses. We are not all the same. This also pertains to when you are calling on customers. Each customer has a different want or need. They may be in a different mindset the day you call on them when they say no.

The truth is that no matter what you are selling, you can sell it anywhere and anytime. The day you make a sale is the day you get paid. Customers are everywhere. But do you just want a customer or do you want repeat business? If you take one customer and build rapport where they become a repeat customer, and do this with the next customer, in no time all you will have is business. I guess the difference between me and the next guy is all mental. I truly believe that is where it all starts. If you believe you can't sell, you can't, and if you think you can sell, you can. If you have done your job right you can ask for the order. The goal isn't to just get a customer, the goal is to keep the customer and make that customer your number one fan so they will refer you to someone else. If you get a "no," go back and build more rapport with that customer. Don't give up because, like I have said before, "no" doesn't necessarily mean "no."

If you want to change something about your business, find a mentor.

If you want to change something about your business, find someone that you trust to help you. Ask someone who is successful if you can go out on the road with them for a day. Watch them in action and model what they do. Find someone to mentor you or hire a sales trainer that will steer you in the right direction and give you the skills to move your business ahead.

New Skill WITHOUT Coaching or Training

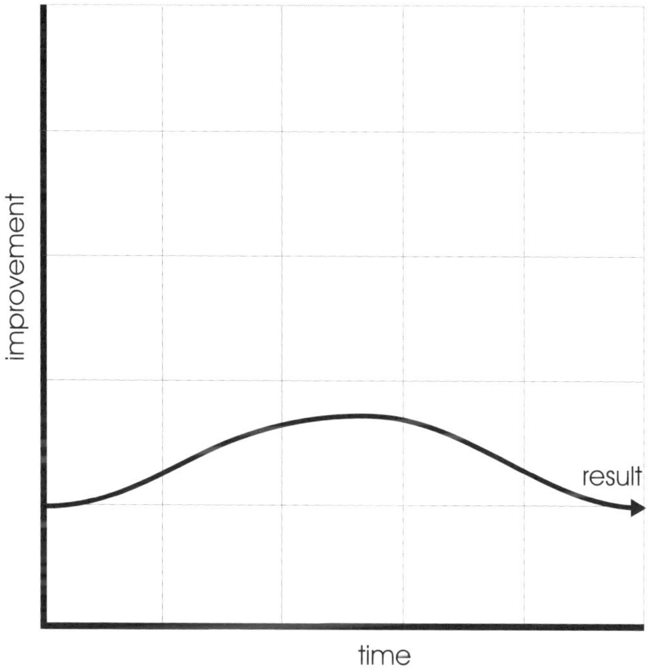

The best training is in the field learning from others who have mastered their business. Barry, from South Africa has been in business for less than six months. He has taken the number one spot in his company for his sales in the past two months. During a call this question was asked: "Has anyone bothered to call Barry in South Africa and find out what he is doing to get the sales?" The answer was a startling "no." Why don't we take the initiative to call those who are more successful than we are? Is it the fear of admitting we want to do better in our business? Here are some key note items:

1. Ask someone you admire in your business if you can go out with them on the road for a day.
2. Find out what they are doing different and implement some of these changes to your business.
3. Ask them lots of questions, but the key is to listen to the answers.
4. Ask a successful person out to lunch and ask them how they became successful…don't say a word, just listen, take notes and model what they are doing.
5. Hire a trainer/coach/mentor to keep you accountable.

If you are looking for better results, unlock the value of coach and mentor — this will improve your skill set.

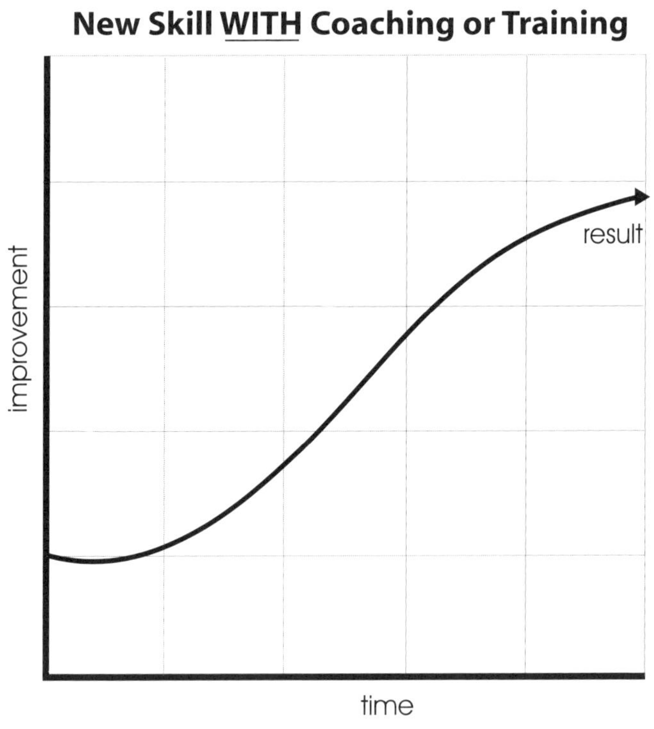

Chapter 15

Accountability

Accountability (n.) - is a concept in ethics with several meanings. It is often used synonymously with such concepts as answerability, enforcement, responsibility, blameworthiness, liability and other terms associated with the expectation of account giving.
-Liable to being called to account, answerable.
-Responsibility to someone or for some activity.
-The state of being accountable, liable or answerable.

Accountability can be enforced by a boss — answering to the expectations of your job. It can, however, be a bit more confusing if you are an entrepreneur. I have often heard the saying, "the good news is that being an entrepreneur you're the boss, and the bad news is that you're the boss..."

> **Good news is that you're the boss, the bad news is... you're the boss.**

We can look at being accountable in three areas in sales and business:

1. **Establishing your responsibilities and expectations.**

   An example would be if you start work at 8:00am and finish at 4:30pm. You show up at work at 8:00am, then get your coffee, return to your desk, turn on your computer, talk to your co-workers and before you know it, it's 8:30. At 4:15pm, you start closing things down so you can be out of the office right at 4:30. What does start and finish time mean?

In this example there are 45 minutes of time that are not productive. Are you being accountable to time or taking advantage of it? When you work for yourself, especially at home, you can get misled many times during the day with unplanned distractions. (Okay I'll throw in a load of laundry in or go get my hair cut before lunch) If you are a sales person on the road and have a daily quota of calls to make do you make up calls on your sheet so it looks good even though you didn't make the quota?

We all share the same number of hours in a day. Why is it that some people use time wisely and others waste time and don't take advantage of it. Where do you see yourself? How can you be accountable to time? I am responsible for everything that happens to me during the day. If I have a problem, I caused it either by my inaction, my reaction or my action. Make a clear path to your time calendar and set boundaries for yourself. Respond to your voice messages and emails in a timely manner. Keep all appointments and agreements. Take the time to follow up on customers and prospects. Remember, the fortune is in the follow up.

The fortune is in the follow-up

A simple and effective tool is to keep a time log. Write down specific times that you want to complete a task or make appointments.

6:00am - 7:00am	- Gym
7:00am - 8:00am	- Shower, breakfast
8:00am - 9:00am	- Return emails and open mail
9:00am - 12:00pm	- Prospect Calls
12:00pm - 1:00pm	- Lunch - pick up dry cleaning
1:00pm	- Follow up appointment with _______
2:30pm	- Follow up appointment with ________
4:00pm - 5:00pm	- Follow up phone calls
5:00pm	- Dinner and family time
7:30 pm	- Check emails and plan for next day

Use the selling time to be selling, not opening the mail or sending emails. Use down time early in the morning or later in the evening to do such tasks. Hold yourself accountable to your time. You can never get wasted time back.

2. Reporting and measuring the results of your performance.

Measure on a daily basis and set the standard for the result you want to accomplish. Again, if you work for yourself, it is important to measure your results so you know where you need to improve your performance. In sales, what did you sell last week, last month, last year and how much more do you have to sell this week to beat your previous performance? Keeping your stats up to date will keep you on track and it will push you to do more. I can tell you what I sold in April of 1988 at the touch of my computer keys. I check my stats often and always aim to increase my sales. Don't get me wrong, there are many times I record my stats and am in disbelief that I am way under my goal. The important thing is that I have looked at them and know what I need to do this week, month and year to do better. You can track your stats in different categories:

- Sales
- Number of Calls
- Number of Conversations
- Number of Appointments
- Cost of Inventory

If you are struggling, ask for help. Have a work buddy that you can practice your presentation with. Have a contest with a fellow worker to motivate yourself to increase your production.

3. Evaluate how you are doing.

Analyze the information and do a performance review of your activities. Be honest with yourself. Then you can make changes to your plan to increase your sales. A group of us were out making cold calls one day and we all met up for lunch. One of the fellows did a pitch to the restaurant owner before we got there. Then, during lunch, we asked the owner if we could ask him a question once the rush was over. He came over nearing the end of our lunch and we asked what he thought of the presentation. Did he want to know more about us and would he be interested in doing business with us based on our presentation? We asked him to be totally honest with us. It was a great experience for all of us. Sometimes we need to just ask how we are doing.

If you have been in the same business for a long time, you may be cutting your presentation short to just get it over with and that can be an explanation for your numbers. If you skim over details or shortcut your presentation because you have done it so many times that you are bored with it, you will lose sales. Remember, every presentation is new to your client. So give it some enthusiasm and don't cut it short. In many cases, all you have to do is ask a direct question to get your evaluation.

Every presentation is new to your customer

If you haven't had the results you want so far this year, it is time to be accountable and stop justifying reasons why not. Make the decision to take action and make up for lost sales. If you are in a leadership role, you need to be responsible for products, decisions, policies, actions and administration. Leaders need to be accountable on many levels because they need to explain and be answerable for results.

In sales, you need to be accountable to your presentation. With a polished and practiced presentation you will face fewer objections.

And let's face it, when your presentation is polished, your customer won't even realize they are getting a sales pitch. When your presentation is polished and perfected you won't need to close, it will automatically happen.

By being accountable to your sales you will believe in what you are doing. You will take the opportunity to ask people for their business and not see it as a risk to do so. Plus you will be able to pull yourself out of a slump and continue to make more sales.

Think of closing a sale like going through the checkout at the grocery store. You put things on the conveyor belt and when you get to the end the only question you are asked by the cashier is "how would you like to pay today; check, credit card, debit or cash?" The cashier isn't wondering if you are going to buy it all, she is confident about your purchase.

The moral of the story is you need to show accountability in all aspects of your business but especially to yourself. You are accountable for your results. Why not develop and use all of the talent God has given you. Don't let your present results control your thoughts and actions. Change your attitude and you will change your income.

Chapter 16

Look Like You Mean Business

I was eating lunch at a busy restaurant and as I looked around the restaurant I wondered if the people were on vacation, out to lunch on their day off or on a working lunch. After careful observation, some people that were dressed like they were on vacation were clearly on a working lunch. In sales, the first place that we need to be accountable is in how we dress and present ourselves on the outside. Look at the people around you and try to speculate who they are and what it is they do for a living. Does what they wear reflect their personality? Personally I know that when I am dressed for business I'm in a professional mode, I accomplish a lot more and make more sales. If you want to promote your business and increase sales, it is important to understand how to dress for business.

How you dress does depend on the job. In sales, it is more about what your customer wants to see. But no matter where you work, be accountable for how you look. Even if you have a landscaping company and work outside in the dirt, a pressed golf shirt and shorts with mud on them still shows that you take the time to look after yourself. A few years ago I was renovating a house. Even though it was filthy I still had my hair done with makeup and a pair of my company earrings on. I ended up selling a pair, like I was wearing, to a neighbor who loved them, even though I was covered in paint.

The Queen of England is reported to have told Prince Charles, "Dress gives one the outward sign from which people can judge the inward state of mind. One they can see, the other they cannot." Clearly, she was saying what many people are reluctant to accept; that people judge us by the way we dress. In all situations, business and social, our outward appearance sends a message.

"Dress gives one the outward sign from which people can judge the inward state of mind."

A woman should be noticed for who she is and her professional skills rather than for what she wears. Her business wear should be appropriate for her industry and her position or title within the industry.

In men's clothing, fashion does not change significantly from season to season but business attire is about being professional and not about being fashionable. It's about presenting yourself in a way that makes your clients feel comfortable and confident with you. Dressing for success is still the rule.

Chapter 17

Get Out of Your Own Way

One of the most frightening times of my life was the day I handed in my resignation at the large steel manufacturing company I worked at. I had been employed at my first full-time job for 11 years. During every performance review I told my boss that I wanted to be selling steel but at that time there were no women on the road selling. Due to this matter, I decided to quit and become an entrepreneur. Everyone in my life, except my husband, thought I was crazy for leaving the "security" of my job. I was paid well and had 5 weeks vacation. That was 20 years ago.

Since making that decision I have made millions, I have won everything you can imagine for my sales and I have as many weeks vacation in a year as I want to take. The money has come, but that wasn't my drive. My drive was to give great customer service and appreciate every sale no matter how big or small. My goal was to stay home with my two children and have a great career on my terms. I knew on the other hand, that if I poured my energy into myself and my business, working it every day, the sky would be the limit. There was no capping my salary, my potential or my growth. I built a great team and have helped thousands change their lives by showing them the way.

Twenty years ago, I remember my first show for my Direct Sales business. I was terrified. I lost my wording, couldn't remember the details and stumbled through my presentation. It felt like it was 150 degrees that night. From that point on I made a decision to sell from my heart. It didn't matter what words I used. What mattered was my passion for selling. Once I took this direction, my sales soared and I became the top sales person in the company. What I want to leave you with from this section follows:

Serve first. I never went out to a show thinking of how much money I was going to make. I always went out thinking about what I can do for my customer and how I can make a difference to them. What's in it for them and not what's in it for me! People can smell commission-breath a mile away. I wanted them to feel great about their purchase.

I believed in what I was selling. Do you believe that the product or service that you are providing is the best in the world?

Are you passionate about your business? Passion is contagious and will reflect to your customers, making them more likely to be interested in what you have to offer. Have fun with your business. Get excited about it.

Are you telling everyone you know about your business? I have met so many people in "sales" but they aren't telling anyone about what they are selling. They stay with the same old crowd and never get out of their comfort zone. Ask, ask and ask again. They say it takes 10 no's to get a yes. Remember this, "no" isn't forever, "no" may be for right this second. "Yes" may be just around the corner. In a selling situation when the answer is "no", always ask the potential customer when it would be a good time to call them back. Even if it is a year down the road, log it in your day timer and be sure to call them back. Follow up is very important and follow through will keep your sales rising. They aren't saying "no" to you, they are saying no to the situation. Expand your horizons. Get out there, join networking groups, meet new people and do some market research.

Follow up is very important and Follow through will keep your sales rising.

Chapter 18

Why Network?

Networking is one of the best opportunities you will have to build relationships, grow professionally and make connections with like-minded people.

Think of what you want to accomplish by joining a networking group. It may be to find a job, meet business owners in your field, expand your contacts or for social reasons. It is important to get involved in regular meetings and club activities that give you the opportunity to mingle with the crowd. This is a time to meet people you may not otherwise have the opportunity to meet.

Build relationships, grow professionally, and connect with like-minded people.

Before joining a networking meeting, you can research the club on their website and find out if it's for you. What is their purpose and mission? How many meetings are you required to attend? What is the cost? What types of events do they hold?

I was at a Chamber of Commerce luncheon recently. I have been a member for years now and it was at this luncheon I took notice that some people stay with the same group of people at all Chamber events. For instance, if they are members of the bank, they sit at the same table or if they are from the City, they sit with their fellow workers. I have always done the opposite. I never sit beside someone I know. I went to the luncheon with my husband and when we got there, we said, "I'll meet you when it is over." You see, why would I sit with my husband when we are both there to meet other business owners? The art of networking is so simple. You may be shy and not like talking to people. If this is you, you are in the right spot at networking meetings. At this particular meeting I went up to a man, extended my hand and said, "Hi I'm Lori." He said, "Thank you for coming up to me, this is my first meeting and I don't know anyone.:"I welcomed him and showed him where I was sitting and asked if he wanted to join me. We ended up having a very nice lunch while getting to know each other's businesses.

The art of networking is simple.

If you watch the traits of people at networking events it is quite interesting. There are people who go straight to the food. There are people who stand with their backs to the wall. There are people you talk to who glance from side to side and over your head looking for a better person to talk to and there are people who remain in the comfort zone of their own group.

Networking is the time to make quality contacts; it isn't a contest to see how many business cards you can get at the event. You will get better results by making a few connections than by simply handing out a dozen business cards with no conversation. There are also people who just go and sit at the table waiting for the lunch to be served. Then there are people who are working the room, taking initiative to meet new people and find out about their business. Let's face it, that is why we go to networking meetings, to meet other like-minded people.

If you aren't a member of a networking group, there are so many to choose from. There are BNI (Business Network International) groups, Chamber of Commerce, Rotary, Lions Club, and Kiwanis to name a few. There are also a lot of independent networking groups. If you can't find one you like, why not start your own group.

When meeting people, watch their non-verbal body language, facial expressions, eye contact and body movement. Be sure to use the person's name, that you met, as quickly as you can during your conversation. This will help you to remember their name. Have a firm handshake, smile and listen to what they are saying. If appropriate, compliment them. Be professional and be yourself. Ask them questions about their business. This is the time to take the focus off yourself by first listening to the other person.

You want to remain professional at all times, which means not consuming too much alcohol if it is served at the event. You want people you meet to remember you as confident, capable and professional.

Dress for business at these events. Remember impressions are made in the blink of an eye.

Impressions are made in the blink of an eye.

At the end of a networking event where there is a keynote speaker, I always go up and introduce myself. I have invited speakers out to lunch so I can learn more about them and tell them about myself, if there is a fit. Some of these meetings have turned into future business deals. This is where the pitch for your business comes into play. Know what you are going to say and have it polished. Always finish your pitch with a question such as: "Does this sound like something you would be interested in?"

Have you ever come home after a networking meeting and put the business cards on your desk? Then, you go to another networking meeting and do the same thing and before you know it you have cards all over the place and you forget which card came from which meeting? Here is a hint that has helped me over the years...

I have a journal book and when I finish an "introductory call" or a networking event, I immediately glue or tape the business card in my journal book on the left side of the page and write a note on the right hand side of the page. I write who I spoke to, the date and something personal I would remember about the person I met, along with a summary of our conversation. I now have all the information in one spot when I follow up with them. When I am finished with that contact, I highlight a big yellow check mark through the page so I know I have followed up.

The day after I meet people at a networking meeting, I send them a hand written note. The professionalism is always noted and it opens the door for follow up and referrals. It lets the person know that I am interested in them and I am committed to success — mine and theirs.

So why network?

What is my payoff?

What value will going to a networking event bring me and the people I meet?

What support do I need to attend the networking meeting?

What skills do I need to network?

What experience can I gain from going to a networking meeting?

Values

Networking requires that you step outside of your comfort zone. Strong relationships will be built over time. The reason to network is to connect with people with similar interests, meet those you can help and find people that can be of help to you.

Support

You need the support of your business, team members, family, customers and your potential customers — including those that you meet at networking events. It is all about building rapport with people and as you get to know others, you will be pleasantly surprised at how much support is there for you.

Skills

Networking is positively impacted by making a good first impression. Professionals are busy people and they value time. Success in sales is about continual networking. Once you have mastered the skill of networking and building rapport with people, you will be able to become a master of sales.

Experience

The experience gained from networking meetings is; how to present your business in a short concise pitch, how to promote your product or service, how to build rapport with like minded people, how to showcase your product, knowledge from keynote speakers and the insight gained from other attendees.

During a major snow storm, I was in a parking lot and decided there was a networking opportunity at hand. I noticed a pick up truck with a snow plow attached to the front. I approached the driver and asked if he plowed private driveways — as I was on my way to shovel my dad's driveway. The man said no, as they only did commercial contracts. I explained to him that my dad's driveway had an enormous amount of snow at the end of the driveway. He asked where my dad lived and the house number and told me he would go and do it for me. I asked him how much I can pay him and he wouldn't take any money. A short while later when I drove to my dad's, the driveway was clear. The good Samaritan had helped me. If I wasn't able to sell myself or network, would he have done the driveway? No. Sales and networking are a part of everything we do.

Sales and networking are a part of everything we do.

Chapter 19

Patterning Your Success

The secret to success in any business is the development of a pattern that can be executed successfully, time and time again. Every business has a sales cycle, which is the sequence of steps that a customer goes through when deciding to buy something.

It is vital to have your sales cycle simplified and established from the customer's perspective so that it generates the desired end result — the sale.

I have successfully used a simple 8 step pattern for sales. These are the action steps for success in sales:

1. **Who** - find someone who needs and wants your product or service.
2. **Connect** - know what to do next and get more leads.
3. **Present** - communicate your product or service.
4. **Close** - confidently make the sale.
5. **Follow Up** - deliver on the deal.
6. **Follow Through** - continue the relationship.
7. **Generate More Business**- ask for referrals and a testimonial.
8. **Repeat the Pattern** - repetition is the key.

WHO
CONNECT
PRESENT
CLOSE
FOLLOW UP
FOLLOW THROUGH
GENERATE MORE BUSINESS
REPEAT
SALES CYCLE

Chapter 20

Step 1 - Who

Find someone who needs and wants your product or service.

Prospects are your resource or raw material for your business. As long as there are prospects, you are in business. So who are your prospects? Is there only a special niche prospect for your product or service or is everyone a candidate?

Your prospect pool is a valuable commodity. How should you treat a valuable commodity? Since this is the first step in the sales cycle, we better do a good job and kick things off right. Here are some very important tips for your list of prospects — the potential people who you may be doing business with:

1. Write your list of prospects down on a list or in your planner — don't keep them in your head.
2. Continually add to your list of prospects (the sales cycle will help you with this).
3. Do not make decisions for your prospects before you've connected with them — don't prejudge.
4. Keep old lists for future reference.

Your prospect list is a renewable resource — renewable only by you!

Your prospect list is a renewable resource — renewable only by you!

Here is a challenge for you. In a five mile radius of your home or office, visit companies or people in your area, introduce yourself and tell them that your business is in the area. Let them know that you would like to find out a little bit about them and their business. You will be amazed at the results you will get. Remember, it's not about your results at this point and it is not about making a sale. The goal of this process is to build rapport. Go into their world first and find out about them. If there is a fit, you have just found yourself a new customer. The same process can be used for simply meeting people if your product or service is not geared for companies.

Call on the people that you give business to. Here are a few examples, your lawyer, accountant, hair stylist, dentist, grocer, coffee shop owner, dry cleaner, car dealer or florist to name a few. We spend a lot of money on services like these; however, many times we don't think to ask them if they know anyone that would be interested in our business. Ask your friends if they could refer you or recommend someone you could call on about your product or service.

Be interested, not interesting.

In closing, I want to leave you with a very important tip. I used to get in trouble in school for doing this and now I get paid very well to do it. Open your mouth and talk to as many people as you can. Be interested not interesting. Go for it, you've got absolutely nothing to lose. Sometimes you just need to get out of your own way.

Chapter 21

Step 2 - Connect

Know what to do next and get more leads

Step two of the sales cycle is to Connect. Connect with your prospect and continue the process of moving through the sales cycle. This is the step that usually involves conquering our fears.

If you always do what you always do, you will always have what you always get. Rise to the challenge, be strong and brave and be your absolute best. Take risks. All you need to do to go after more business is to simply ask for it! Be consistent in what needs to be done.

To go after more business, simply ask for it!

I have seven activities you can do to generate more leads quickly. These activities will apply equally well in your business and for your clients. Use them to get you in motion, then correct, make adjustments and complete the activity again.

1. Cold Calling

There are two different types of Cold Calling — phone calling and on-site visits. Both can be very powerful if used properly and they both require fairly high levels of confronting fears. It is extremely important to recognize three important points before you begin Cold Calling of any type. First, this is more about creating motion and putting energy into the sales system than in creating tons of leads. When selling efforts are made in high volume, business starts to appear — albeit, not necessarily as a direct result of the calls themselves. When energy is put out in selling, sales manifest themselves in many different forms. The second is that this actually has more to do with personal therapy and conquering fears than generating leads. Cold Calls are a hotbed of battling that inner voice inside your head. Use Cold Calling as a chance to take control of that inner voice. Third, the results are often 10:1 (No: Yes) or worse when cold calling. Don't be discouraged. Focus on your progress and keep exposing the business.

When energy is put out in selling, sales manifest themselves in many different forms.

a) Phone Cold Calling:

- Just do it. Don't give yourself the excuse not to. Master that inner voice inside your head and make the calls.
- Know your purpose. Have a clear outcome and tune your message accordingly. Going for a 'close' on the first cold call may not be the best idea. However, this may differ depending on the product or service.
- Build and practice your script before you call. Building an interest-grabbing script means being respectful and explaining the notion of the call very concisely — then end with a question. The question is critical to creating further dialog, otherwise the call may end abruptly.
- Speak with the right person. Only the right person can say "yes," but just about anyone in the business can say "no" and end your call. Get the right decision maker and then give them your pitch.
- Debrief. If possible, review your results and practice your pitch with someone who can offer meaningful feedback (generally someone who has done it before).

Find out what works and what needs to be changed (if anything). Keep in mind, that sometimes what needs to change is simply the volume of calls. Three calls a day is not considered motion — you don't have enough feedback to allow you to correct.

- Measure. Keep your statistics. Without data you are just another opinion. If you make ten calls and only speak with two people and one of them is interested, your results are not a 10% success — you are getting a 50% success rate! Make sure you have meaningful numbers including how many calls you have made, how many people you have spoken with, what the results of the conversations were, how many converted into sales, how long it took and what was the average unit of sale.
- Have a follow up system. You won't reach everyone the first time. You need a system to follow up on leads. It should be a database list, but that doesn't mean it has to be complicated. Make sure you have a system of following up on outstanding leads.
- Next steps. Ensure that you create a reason to follow up and reconnect. Create an excuse to send additional information or follow up with a call, something to provide you with a way back in.
- Smile — people can hear it in your voice when you're not smiling on the phone. Have a mirror in front of you so you can see your facial expressions — a smile on your face generates a whole new energy on the phone.

b) On-Site Cold Calling:

- All of the elements of telephone cold calling apply, plus there are a few other issues that must be considered.
- Look the part. Your dress and deportment are critical as you'll be managing a blink reflex when you walk into someone's office. This includes clothing, personal hygiene, body odor, cologne, your energy level, your smile and much more.
- The Handshake — your handshake must be a good one.

Here are the secrets to a successful handshake:

- *Web to Web — the web between your thumb and index finger must connect with the web between their thumb and forefinger.*
- *Firm grasp, but don't hurt them.*
- *Make eye contact.*
- *Smile.*
- *One or two pumps of the arm, but not dramatically.*
- *Be present.*
- *"Hi, I'm ___________."*

- Show appreciation and respect for their time.
- Find something to connect with them — comment on a photo on their desk, cleanliness of the office, the business itself… some point of rapport.

2. Direct Mail

Direct mail programs are lead generation tools that involve sending some sort of printed material to a contact and attempting to elicit further interest. They may use flyers, post cards, brochures or sales letters. We'll focus on sales letters in this instance.

A favorite process is to start by creating a "special report." Write a short but useful report that will provide value to the prospect. Then, craft your sales letter around announcing the report and giving instructions for how to request the report. This is a very powerful process because the prospects that request the report are volunteering for further contact. It is important to send the report immediately or make it available on the Internet right away, and it is also important to ensure that you can track who has requested it and who has not.

In the report, include a free telephone consultation where you will address as many issues or questions as possible in the 20 minutes and commit to not using it as a selling call.

What happens is that by the time someone calls you, they have volunteered three times — read your letter, ordered the report, requested the consultation — and the odds of closing that prospect are extremely high.

Understand that the response rates in Direct Mail programs are very low — 2-3%, so ensure you approach a market that is big enough to create statistically relevant results.

Also ensure that you test the headline of your letter. Small changes in wording can create dramatically different results.

Finally, track your numbers and ensure that you have a follow up system. Consider blending your direct mail and cold calling program to follow up the sales letter with a phone call.

3. Referrals

Getting referrals is a great way to generate leads. The problem is that most businesses don't have a process or discipline to getting referrals.

Here are a few ideas for you:

- Know what a good client is and be able to describe it to your customers so that they know who they should refer to you.
- After doing work for a client, send them a thank you note and a request for a referral.
- Always send thank you notes for referrals made, even if the leads don't turn into business.
- Target the top 20 clients of your top 20 clients. We tend to do business with people like us. That means that your clients likely do business with people like you. Work to get access to your clients' best clients.
- Warn them. When you sign a deal with a client, tell them right then and there that it is your goal that they will be so happy with your work they will gladly give you three good leads when the project is over. Somewhere along the way,

your client will tell you how happy they are with how things are progressing. When they do, remind them that you'll be asking for those referrals after the project. When the project is done, they will often have the leads ready for you when you ask, and then no one is surprised when you bring up the idea of referrals.

- Even when cold calling and someone says "no," ask them if they know anyone else who might be able to take advantage of what you are offering. You might be surprised at the results!

4. Public Speaking

Get exposure to as many people as possible. One of the most efficient ways to do this and to leverage your time is by being at the front of a room. Present in as many locations and in front of as many people as possible. Consider having copies of your Special Report or something free handy to give out. That way you can have a draw and get the names and numbers of everyone in the room.

Use Public Speaking as an opportunity to enroll people further so that they shift from being contacts to prospects. Where do you go to public speak? Join some networking groups, Chamber of Commerce, Rotary, Lions Club, Kiwanis, to name a few. Then you can offer to speak at their breakfast or luncheon meeting on your topic.

5. Frequency Program

> Frequency of interaction with prospects and customers keeps the relationship going.

The purpose of frequency programs is to maintain business while offering 'top of the mind' for your prospects, create channels for extending offers as well as generating both leads and sales. Frequency of interaction with your prospects and customers keeps the relationship going.

Frequency programs should occur at

least once per month and should always include “value added” information for your reader. This does not necessarily mean that the information must be about what you are offering — it should address whatever is on the mind of your prospect, whatever is keeping them awake at night. Every other message should include an offer of some sort or you will end up conditioning your client to get something for nothing. A newsletter or broadcast email is ideal. There are many online services available now which provide templates, tracking, opt-in and opt-out tools, protection against spam and much more.

6. Joint Venture

Find organizations that are doing business with your target market and create opportunities to work together. Come up with ways that would be valuable for the other company to give you access to their client list or even refer you to their clients.

7. Trade Shows

Trade shows are challenging because you must be very precise in order to get meaningful results. It's not about how many people attend a trade show, it's how many of your target market are at the trade show? Focus on business-to-business trade shows and recognize that the vendors may be the targets for your business, rather than the attendees. You can pursue the vendors, but only if you are extremely brief and do your real pitch later in a follow-up.

Image is everything at a trade show, so ensure that you control the space very carefully. This includes how you look, what you say, what your booth looks like, how tidy and garbage-free it is. You must be professional at all times and must have an approach prepared and practiced in advance. Finally, all follow-ups from the show should be completed within one week of the tradeshow for maximum results.

Chapter 22

Step 3 - Present

Communicate your product or service.

Now that we have talked about the first two steps of the sales cycle, the next step is an important one — presenting to your prospective customer. This involves your formal presentation, connecting with them, asking questions, solving their challenges, negotiating and communicating effectively your product or service.

After working your way through the connecting step and lead generation activities, the defining moment is when you schedule an appointment and truly model your expertise. The appointment is critical to your success.

With your business in place, the next thing to do is gain immediate exposure. If you have come into the market as a relative unknown or from non-existence, here the steps to use to make yourself known:

1. Find out what is needed and wanted.
2. Learn the lay of the land, who communicates with who.
3. Serve!

Learn what is happening in your community. Listen to what is needed and wanted. Become a member of your Chamber of Commerce, trade organizations, community action groups, networking groups and business owner forums. Volunteer for everything. Get known through your actions, not your words.

Ask lots of questions. Physically walk your territory and personally meet as many business owners and key managers as you can. This should be part of your daily and weekly routine and should never end. Do not worry so much about selling. Spend your time asking, probing, learning and showing genuine interest. Communicate. Inform them that you are new in the business or tell them about your company. Let them know that you are there to serve in any way that you can. If you do this exercise, your business will be sure to grow. You will be amazed at how many businesses you didn't even know existed in a mere few blocks of your home. By asking questions and entering "their world" this will create conversation. If they are not interested or do not need your service at the time, ask another question, "Could you refer me to anyone who could use my product or service?"

Ask questions and enter "their world," this will create conversation.

Here are the habits that I practice in order to create the best possible appointment.

1. Be Early

Fifteen minutes early to be precise. Now, this doesn't necessarily mean walking into the client's office 15 minutes before your appointment, because that can prove to be as frustrating to a prospect as your being late. If you schedule your time to arrive 15 minutes early, then you will be able to more comfortably negotiate any delays that may appear on your way there. The stress stays low and you stay in control. Get to their office 15 minutes early and then use that time effectively. Use it to review what you'll be presenting, practice your pitch, mentally step into their shoes and consider what you'll be saying from their perspective.

2. Dial up Your Energy Level

Before you enter the client's office, you must increase your energy level. There is a general principle that when you bring two people together in a selling situation, the one with the highest energy wins. You can listen to a motivational or instructional CD, change your state physically or whatever it is you need to do to walk in with high energy and the right frame of mind.

3. Do Some Sales Homework

Review the training or motivational CDs that have the most pertinent information to what you think you'll be encountering so that the content is fresh in your mind.

4. Look the Part

Your dress and demeanor is critical. You need to model your expertise and show your prospect what a professional salesperson looks like, smells like, talks like and moves like. The personal space you create will generate a blink reaction in the first few seconds — be the leader.

5. The Handshake

Your handshake must be a good one. Remember the secrets to a successful handshake that we discussed earlier.

6. Create Rapport

Rapport is made up of three elements — Shared Reality (you're in the same meeting), Affinity (common liking and interest), and Communication. Generate Rapport by having a sincere interest in the client and what is important to them.

7. Focus on Their Needs

You are there to serve the client's needs, so focus on them and allow the individual to express themselves fully. Question the client so that you have a true appreciation of the value, extent and costs of the challenges they are facing.

8. Ask Questions, Ask Questions, Ask Questions!

The only way to be fully present and arrive at the truth of what your client is facing is to ask questions. There are three major categories of questions you can ask your clients. Here are examples for each:

Information Gathering:

- What prompted you/your company to look into this?
- What are your expectations or requirements for this product or service?
- What process did you go through to determine your needs?
- How do you see this happening?
- What is it that you'd like to see accomplished?
- With whom have you had success in the past?
- With whom have you had difficulties in the past?
- Can you help me understand that a little better?
- What does that mean?
- How does that process work now?
- What challenges does that process create?
- What challenges has that created in the past?
- What are the best things about that process?
- What other items should we discuss?

Qualifying:

- What do you see as the next action steps?
- What is your timeline for implementing/purchasing this type of service/product?
- What other data points should we know before moving forward?
- What budget has been established for this?
- What are your thoughts?
- Who else is involved in this decision?
- What could make this no longer a priority?
- What's changed since we last talked?
- What concerns do you have?

Establishing rapport, trust & credibility:
- How did you get involved in… ?
- What kind of challenges are you facing?
- What's the most important priority to you? Why?
- What other issues are important to you?
- What would you like to see improved?
- How do you measure that?

9. Go Where the Room Needs to Go

What I mean by this is don't be constrained by your agenda. Follow what the people in the room need to address. It might be you and one other person, or a whole committee of people — but there will be needs in that room that are different than what you expected. Follow those needs and serve the client. Be ready to adapt.

10. Practice, Practice and More Practice

Success in sales comes with practice. Drill yourself with the common questions and objections that customers will have so that the answers will come to you naturally when you are presenting.

Chapter 23

Step 4 - Close

Confidently make the sale

Always be closing!

On every call a sale can be made. Either you close the client on how they can benefit from your product or service, or they close you on why they can't. Either way, a sale is made. In business we just have to decide who is going to close. Don't you want it to be you making the sale, rather than the client turning the sale down?

Either you close or your customer closes you on why you can't. Either way, a sale is made!

Everything you do from the moment you arrive early until all the follow ups are done — are all closing efforts. What do you want the outcome to be? Isn't it to close the deal?

Sometimes we are just afraid to ask for the sale. What holds us back from asking? Fear of rejection, fear of success, fear of doing the work? Sometimes we are just afraid to go after the opportunities that are right in front of us.

Before you go in for the close, remember to always anchor your past successes. Have you closed a deal before? The answer is yes, so there should be no reason why you can't close now. Take your right hand as you are reading this and make that fist, give it the pump and say "yes!" I know you are sitting there right now thinking, Lori, you can't be serious, but yes I am. Anchoring your success before you go in for a close instills confidence in yourself. If we are confident, then we can close.

I want to share an experience that I just had in a closing.

I was at a yacht club helping our friend sell raffle tickets. There was a man way down at the last dock and I said, "I will go and sell him one." My friend said "No don't bother, he is miserable, doesn't talk to anyone, complains about everything and doesn't ever participate in club activities." That was all I needed. I said, "I'll be right back." The raffle was for a collapsible cooler bag and it was filled with bottled water left over from the yacht club function we had the night before. I said hello to the man, asked what he was cooking on his BBQ and showed him the great cooler bag which would be perfect for his boat. I asked him if he could use something like this. I then opened it and said, "If you win you get all this free bottled water." He looked at me and I then let him know that the tickets were only 3 for $5.00. "Would you be interested in purchasing some?", I asked. He looked at his wife and said, "Go get the money."

I could hear the sigh coming from my friends and all the yacht club members. They couldn't believe that I got the sale. My friend then offered me any amount of money I wanted to come and work for him because he couldn't believe what he just saw.

You see, it isn't always about the sale at first. It is about the thought, then the action, then the result that comes from the particular action.

THOUGHT ➔ ACTION ➔ RESULT

I could have agreed and said, "okay, I won't go and try to sell him something," based on their experiences or, I could have said, "I'm going to try anyways." I chose to give it a try. After all what did I have to lose? How many times have you listened to someone else's advice and not gone in to make a sale based on their results?

It is about making a good first impression, being confident, connecting with the client, knowing your presentation, showing the benefit of your product or service to the customer, offering something free and then going for the close. Most of all, it is having the intention of the sale first and not being afraid of the "no." Asking questions is the key.

Win Win

This is a big subject and addresses many issues. For the moment, to keep it simple, consider this. If the client doesn't receive great value from you, then they don't win. If you aren't properly compensated for the work, then you don't win. It is not a sale unless there is an exchange of value (your services for a check). Anything less is called charity, not sales. Appreciate your own value; create value for the client and everyone wins.

Keep the door open. The client may say "No." Your job is to at least create reasons and opportunities for future contact. Offer to send them some information and then follow up. Add them to your email frequency program and then follow up. Find some other information after the fact that they would find useful and then follow up.

> Your customer may say "No." Your job is to create reasons and opportunities for future contact.

Always remember to keep the door open. In a selling situation or a closing situation always ask open-ended questions so it isn't a yes or no answer. Be truly interested in your customer, not interesting. Here are some examples of open ended questions. Take note of the beginning words in the sentences and the next time you ask a question try using one of them.

- What type of products do you use?
- When would be a better time to call?
- How many employees do you have?
- Why do you ask?
- How long have you been in business?
- How many services do you offer?
- How can you reduce your outgoing costs?
- How much time do you take off, in a year, from your business?
- How do you see our service helping your business?
- Where do you find the best people to hire?
- When did you last do a business check up?
- Why do you think you are in this situation?
- What is your biggest cost in your business?
- When was the last time you had fun with your employees?
- What services do you outsource at the moment?
- Who is your longest-standing employee?
- What kind of assistance will help you right now?
- What is your niche?
- How accurate are your stats?
- How do you get your financial reports?
- What have you tried to improve in your marketing?
- What strategic plan is in place?
- How is your business going right now?
- Who is your target market?
- What is your one-year plan for your company?
- How do you track your stats?
- What can we bring to the table?

The person who is in control of a sale is the one who is asking the questions.

Once you have put the closing question forward, what do you do next?

During your time with the prospective customer, try to use your judgment about their personality to assess how they will react. Some words to use during closing are "imagine," "picture this" and "do you prefer."

The person in control of the sale is the one asking the questions.

Listen for buying signals such as; "How many have you got left?," "When can you deliver?," "When does the sale end?," "What colour does it come in?" Once you hear these buying signs, stop selling. I have witnessed many closes stop when the person selling doesn't know when to shut up. When the customer starts asking buying questions — listen, answer and stop selling.

Now might be the time to create a sense of urgency. When I was purchasing a new mattress a few weeks ago, the salesman mentioned that the sale ended tomorrow. I asked, "How many do you have in stock?" He was brilliant, he stopped selling and said, "Hang on a minute I will go and check." A few minutes later he came back and said, "One, but we would have to ship it in from another city so it would take a few extra days to deliver." When he said "one" it created a sense of urgency that made me get my credit card out.

Don't be afraid to just simply ask for the sale. The salesman then proceeded to say, "How will you be paying for that, VISA or MasterCard?" I knew that there was only one left and if I wanted it I had better get out my credit card. If he had of said, "Do you want to think about it?" I could have walked.

What he did next was give me a few alternatives. I could put a deposit down on the mattress and receive two free pillows or pay in full now and get a $109.00 mattress pad thrown in, too.

I gave him the objection of "Why don't you just throw that in anyway?" He came back to my objection by saying, "The manager was in the store and wanted me to close the sale so he sweetened the deal since it was the last day." He didn't say another word. He gave me time to decide what I wanted. Once I said, "Okay I'll pay now with my MasterCard," the salesman assured me that I was going to be very happy with my purchase and told me he would follow up with me a day or so before the delivery would take place. He went over the next steps to complete the purchase. He handed me his card and said, "If you need anything else Lori, just call and I will be happy to look after you."

In closing situations a purchase might not be in the person's plans or budget. This might be the sole issue. If you truly believe in your product, know you would provide excellent service and the product would benefit the individual or company, ask the customer whether they would proceed if the money for your product was in their budget? If they say "yes," sincerely tell them that you are glad to see the benefit your product or service would have on their business. Also remember, that a "no" may not be a "no" forever. Before leaving, you could ask when a better time would be to call on them again. There is a difference between asking for a sale and helping people make decisions that are good for them.

There have been many times I have walked away from a close due to money issues, but the way I left it with the customer allowed me to come back to them at a later date.

Many salespeople are afraid to close. You have to break through the barrier of that fear of closing because that is when you will make more money.

In direct selling, where I am selling a business, I often stop during my presentation and say this, "Mary, how are you feeling about all of this so far?" If Mary likes it, and I can tell by her questions and facial expression, I move on to close. If she were to give me objections, I would handle her objections before attempting to close. The last thing I want is to make Mary feel pressured and then she will in turn reject me. This can make it a little bit awkward in trying to win her over after such a decline.

Chapter 24

Step 5 - Follow Up

Deliver on the Deal

Okay, so now you have closed the deal and you are jumping up and down in celebration. Before you celebrate too much, now is the time to realize what has just happened. You have closed, congratulations, but that isn't where it stops. That is the starting point to developing a relationship with your new customer. At a sales seminar I asked some people what "delivering on the deal" meant to them. Most answered with this statement, "Who cares, you closed so delivering is no big deal."

Delivering is the key to securing future business. It doesn't matter if you are delivering a product, service or a presentation. It's what comes in the package that counts!

Sales = confidence + technique = congruence

Technique is important when you deliver but you have to have confidence if you are going to succeed in sales. Listening to someone deliver who has no confidence is not only painful to you, but to the presenter as well. How do you get confidence in what you are delivering? — practicing your technique over and over and over until you are confident. When you are confident you will be congruent and this will attract business.

In selling a product it is all about delivering with style. The way you wrap up the purchase, the tissue paper, the ribbon, the gift bag.

If you take the time to do small extra details, your customer will want you back!

Most times, the packaging gets the customer more excited than the product you sold. Does it take more time to package this way? Yes it does. Is it worth your time and the few cents it costs for the tissue paper and ribbon? Absolutely! If you take the time to do small extra details, your customer will want you back!

If you go into a high end gift store, they wrap everything in tissue and then put it in a big bag, making you feel like you have made a special purchase. This is a win/win for the company as well because you walk out of the store with their name all over the large bag, a walking advertisement.

When I purchased my BMW, on delivery the salesman gave me a gift basket filled with all sorts of goodies. It was cello wrapped and had lots of ribbon, it was beautiful and I was impressed. Will I buy from him again? Yes. He went the extra mile to make me (the customer) happy.

When we purchased our first boat the same thing happened. We were provided with a beautiful gift basket stuffed with nautical items all done up in cellophane and ribbon. Was it expensive for the salesperson to do this? No. Was it worth the salesperson spending money to make money? Yes. Was it worth the salesperson's time to put this together? Yes.

Even though you have just spent thousands and thousands of dollars, the extra incentive at the end of the sale is what you remember.

Companies that offer a free gift with purchase, sell so much because of the free gift. People will actually spend more to get a free gift. I have seen it where someone really doesn't want or need the item but buy it just to get the free gift.

It doesn't matter the cost of the item you are delivering. It can be a $20 item or a multi-thousand dollar commercial or industrial product or service.

Delivering a presentation is no different. Are you prepared? Is your script polished? Are your shoes polished? Are you ready for whatever comes your way? Are you ready to stay longer if needed? Have you done some due diligence on the company you are presenting to so you are ready? Do you thank the company when you are done?

Continue asking questions. Don't assume you know everything. Deal with each individual so they feel free to talk to you openly.

If you want to ensure you receive names from the attendees of your presentation, give away a free book or CD and have them put their business card in for a draw. That way you can keep the contact information after the presentation.

When I was in Phoenix, I had an experience at a restaurant that I'll never forget. The meal was great, the presentation wonderful. However, the one thing that happened which made me want to be a repeat customer was when the owner came over to our table and said, "Thank you for not cooking tonight." I have been to hundreds of restaurants and this is the first time I have ever been thanked for not cooking. Isn't that fantastic?

It is the way you deliver to your customer that will be remembered.

It is the way you deliver to your customer that will be remembered.

After each delivery you make to a customer, there is a critical piece to the puzzle. DEBRIEF.

What worked?
What didn't work?
What did I learn?
What did I learn about myself?

Plan ➡ Action ➡ Debrief ➡ Make Adjustments

If you practice debriefing daily, your results can only go one way and that is **UP!** There is a repeatable process for success. This behavior will ensure improvement and generate the results you are looking for.

> Results come from the things we do — our behaviors.

Results come from the things we do — our **behaviors**.

Chapter 25

Step 6 - Follow Through

Continue the Relationship

Now that you have delivered on the deal, thanking your customer is the key to ending this process. Sending a hand-written thank you note can go a long way in continuing your relationship with your customer. I just read that Doug Conant, the CEO of Campbell's Soup, has written over 16,000 thank-you notes to employees since 2001 — and re-energized the company in the process!

I have been personally thanked for sending a thank you note. That always makes me smile when I get a call thanking me for thanking them. Go the extra mile and buy some great cards, always hand sign them and put a commemorative stamp on the envelope. They are great stamps and cost no more than a normal stamp. It is about making your customer feel special and letting them know you value their business. In today's world we constantly open our mailboxes to find endless amounts of junk mail and bills. Why not make someone's day by sending a thank you card. When I send a thank you card I always put a notation in my card to ask if they would refer me to someone they know (you'll see why shortly...).

Always deliver in person — following through can lead to the next sale.

Sometimes we get so busy that we ship our deliveries instead of delivering them in person. By delivering in person, you can make the next sale or follow up on your last presentation or product delivery. This step does refer to items that are deliverable in person. You wouldn't want to hand deliver a fridge and stove. But if it is attainable to hand deliver it, it gives you the chance to drop in and create more rapport with the client — continuing the relationship.

When I hand deliver something I always call in advance to make sure my contact will be there. I let them know that I will be in town and would like to drop off their order. I then ask if they have a second to see me while I'm there. That is when I follow up, up-sell and cross-sell.

We live in a society where we get so much for so little that we have trouble appreciating value. A lot of times we don't appreciate the value ourselves.

When we follow up, we need to go into the customer's world first and show appreciation for their value. When they feel they get value from what you have given them, they will be more willing to invest in your product or service again.

When following up, be sure to ask a question. Some examples might be:

> Were you happy with the product or service?
> How has this helped your company?
> Would you be interested in being invited to my next _____?
> Can I send you our new catalog when it comes out?
> I just wanted you to know about our new product, do you have time to hear about it now?
> How can I be of service to you in the future?

Keeping your customer in your frequency program is a way of staying in touch and letting them know that you appreciate them. That way when you have a new product flyer or catalog, you can keep in touch. Remember this, selling requires energy. When you put two people together in a selling situation, the person with the highest energy is going to win. The person who follows up and follows through will retain the customer. This leads to up selling and cross selling. Let's say that you were brought into a company to do a two-hour presentation. The up sell could be to come back and do another presentation and the cross sell could be to add a product to sell that would be of benefit to the customer.

Follow up and follow through retains the customer and leads to up selling and cross selling.

I always follow up a few weeks later to ask how my customer liked the product or service. Again, debriefing is important. What worked when you followed up? What didn't work? What did you learn? What did you learn about yourself?

If you are not following up on your customer, ask yourself why not? Maybe you just plain can't be bothered. Remember, the highest energy wins and following up can lead to more and more business. I think that any of the business I have personally lost was due to not following up because I was too busy. I have changed my way of looking at business now and realize times are changing. If you want to keep a customer you have to make your move.

I was recently talking to a real estate agent who shared her experience with me. She told me that an acquaintance of hers was so happy to share the news that she just bought a new house. The agent tried to conceal her shocked expression and refrained from screaming out and asking why she had bought the house from someone else. The acquaintance told her that another agent had called to tell her of this great offer which had just come on the market and asked if she would be interested in seeing it. That was the end of the story. Someone didn't follow up…

How many times might this have happened to you? The moral of this step is to always follow up and stay in touch with your customers. If you want a life-long customer, you have to take the time and have the energy to keep in contact.

Don't be afraid to follow up. This is truly adding value to your product or service. Your customer will be impressed that you followed up and they will remember that for years to come.

Chapter 26

Step 7 - Generate More Business

Ask for referrals and a testimonial.

Generating more business from existing business is the process of endless referrals. This step in the sales cycle is how you can auto-generate more business. Think of it this way. The deal is not done until you have a testimonial or a referral. A successful sale is one that leads you to the next prospect. If you can't get a referral, then ask for a testimonial — testimonials give third party credibility.

> **Testimonials give third party credibility.**

Are you uncomfortable asking for what you want? Your customers will be glad you asked them for a testimonial; after all, they were happy with the service you provided. Who do your customers know that would also love to do business with you?

At my doctor's office they have a sign up on the wall that says, "The highest form of a compliment to our practice is when you refer us to your friends or family."

The power of a testimonial is amazing. Being referred to another person or business is a huge WIN.

What can a testimonial do for you? The list is limitless and here are a few of the highlights:

- Get you repeat business.
- Introduce you to new business.
- Create a file that you keep your testimonials in so you can use them as references.
- Let's you know that "being you" really does work.

One of the reasons most people don't get referrals is simply, they don't ask. Getting a referral is a great way to generate leads. In Step 6, the Follow Through, I suggested sending a thank you card when you have completed your sale. I explained how I always put a notation in the card asking for a referral. Here is an example of what I would write:

> Mary;
>
> I want to thank you for your business and to let you know that I really appreciated it. The program was a real success. I have enclosed a few of my business cards and would really appreciate if you could pass them out to other colleagues. I generate most of my business through repeat and referral business. Thanks for passing my name along.
>
> Also, thank you very much for the testimonial and the two leads you sent my way. I will be following up in the next day or so. Again, thank you for your business.
>
> Lori

As we covered earlier, warn your customer that you aim to please. When you close a deal with a client, why not tell them, right then and there, that it is your goal that they will be so happy with your work they will gladly give you three good leads when the project is over. Somewhere along the way your client will tell you how happy they are with how things are progressing. When they do, remind them that you'll be asking for those referrals after the project. When the project is done, they will often have the leads ready for you when you ask, and then no one is surprised when you bring up the idea of referrals.

Ask, ask, ask.

Three key words to sum up this step…ask, ask, ask. Whenever you are working with a client and they express delight, ask for a written testimonial. They will be more inclined to give references if they have written a testimonial. Here is a sample testimonial that I received:

> Dear Lori;
>
> I wanted to take a moment to express my sincerest gratitude to you for your enormous contribution to the success of my franchise.
>
> For 22 years I owned an advertising agency — I built the agency up to $10 million in annual billings. My life was all about sales. I have studied sales techniques, attended seminars and I thought I knew it all.
>
> The impact of your seminar has had a profound effect on making my franchise the No. 1 BarkBusters franchise in Canada. I outsold all 32 other Canadian franchises — even though I have only been operating for 8 weeks. I have a closing rate of 92% despite the fact that 70% of my potential customers are French speaking!
>
> The referral program I have developed (the most successful in the company history) is a direct result of your seminar. The inner strength and confidence I now have in my business is a direct result of your training. Persistence really does pay off when you go after what you want and stick to your mission.

I attribute a large part of my success to the techniques I learned from you.

Thank you so much for your contribution.

Chapter 27

Step 8 - Repeat the Pattern

Repetition is key.

This wraps up the 8 step sales cycle.

If you follow the selling cycle and use the steps outlined, you will have more business than you ever dreamed of.

The one thing to remember is selling requires energy. What you put in you get back. Don't take short cuts in business but find ways to generate more business with a system that works.

> **What you put in you get back.**

There may be many times when you want to quit, give up and go back to doing the same thing you did before. There is one quality that will guarantee your success and that is the willingness to stick with it — to see it through to the end. Persistence Pays!

Refuse to settle for anything less. Think of sales like a snowball. You may start off slow and small but as you build momentum the sales and customer base will continue to grow. The cycle provides the duplication effect which develops success habits for your business.

The longer you hang in there, the greater the chance that

something will happen in your favor. No matter how hard it seems, the longer you persist, the more likely your success will be.

Your attitude will be the thermostat for your business.

Your attitude will be the thermostat for your business. It affects everything and everyone. Having the right attitude is vital. Here are 12 Steps that I use to protect my attitude and ensure I am giving 100% to my business.

The 12 "Ds":

DESIRE

What do you want?
List two desires that you have for both your business and family.

DETERMINE

What is it going to take?
What changes do you need to make?
What are you willing to do for this period of time to reach your determined goal?

DEFEND

Defend your new position. Know that when you set a big goal, you need to have a positive attitude and be raring to go. Challenges build confidence. There is no gain without pain. Defend your plan for your success!

DEFLECT

Deflect negativity. Understand why people are negative towards your goal. They may want to protect you. They may be afraid that you will be successful in reaching your new goal and that you will leave them behind. Many people are not happy where they are in their life and misery loves company. Maybe they just do not understand. In any event, do not take it personally. Use these comments to motivate you and show them that you can do it.

DELEGATE

You will need help to make the short-term changes that will be necessary to achieve your goal. If possible, encourage your family's involvement in the first three steps, Desire, Decide and Determine. Let them know what is in it for them, how they will benefit and how they can help. People will support what they create.

DELAY

For a short period of time, delay social activities and volunteer work. Inform people that you will not be as available for a short period of time. You are working towards a goal which will improve your life and your family's life, and will give you more time and energy for social and volunteer work, as well as free up additional time for yourself.

DETECT

Self sabotage. Sometimes when fear sets in and we don't think we are going to make our goal, we start rationalizing that we did not really want the goal and the time is not right. Recognize the rationalizing and push through to your goal.

DEMAND

Demand excellence from yourself. This is your goal and you can do it.

DELIGHT

Delight in your accomplishments no matter how small. Celebrate your victories. Remember, experience is what we get when we don't get what we want. The more experience, the more confident you become.

DEVELOP

With all this experience, you are developing into a confident, determined person who can overcome any obstacle. You are developing a future for yourself.

DELIVER

Deliver the promises that you make to your clients, your family and your friends.

DEAL

Make yourself a deal that when your goals start being met, you reward yourself. Set small attainable goals, monthly goals, six month goals, one year goals and five year goals. Keep stats daily and when you get there, CELEBRATE!

Chapter 28

Are You Ready to Break Out of Your Shell?

This past New Year's Eve my husband and I decided to stay in and cook a nice dinner of steak and lobster. My son came home with a live lobster for our feast. It was massive. I wasn't sure how to cook the lobster so I looked it up on the internet.

I wondered how a lobster was able to grow bigger when its shell was so hard. I had to admit that learning how lobsters grew had never been high on my list of priorities. However, now that one was swimming around in my laundry tub, there was a reason…

I read an article on how they grew. The only way the lobster grows is to shed its shell at regular intervals. When its body begins to feel cramped inside the shell, the lobster instinctively looks for a reasonably safe spot to rest while the hard shell comes off and the pink membrane underneath forms the basis of the next shell. But, no matter where the lobster goes for this shedding process, it is very vulnerable. It can get tossed against a coral reef or eaten by a fish. In other words, a lobster has to risk its life in order to grow.

In thinking about this, the lobster can teach us some great life lessons.

We all know when our shells have gotten too tight. We feel angry or depressed or frightened because life is no longer exciting or challenging. We are doing the same old things and beginning to feel bored. Or we find ourselves doing things we hate to do and again feel stifled in our shells.

Some of us continue to smother in old shells that are no longer useful or productive. That way we can at least feel safe and like nothing bad can happen to us. Others are luckier. Even though we know we will be vulnerable to the dangers ahead, we realize that we must take chances or risk suffocating.

> **Rid yourself of your old shell and get ready for bigger and better adventures!**

I invite you to shed your shell. Rid yourself of your old shell despite the dangers and get ready for bigger and better adventures!

The lobster sheds its shell in order to have room for growth the following year. They shed 20 - 25 times in their lifetime. It takes about 6-8 weeks of being at risk until the new shell hardens again. In human life, that is about how long it takes to get comfortable doing something new.

Are you willing to shed your old shell and make room for growth? What have you got to lose?

What are your plans for growth?

Starting your week, month or quarter off with a bang requires focusing your efforts to maximize results.

Eighty percent of your sales come from twenty percent of your customers.

Who are your best customers? Now is the perfect time to contact them about ways you can help start their week, month, quarter or year off with a bang by using your product or service. Maybe it has been awhile since you have been in touch with them. Reconnect with them, thank them for their past business and ask how you can help them today.

Support and encourage the people around you.

Praising your team for their results and encouraging them to reach for the stars will go a long way. If you are in a leadership position, why not take your top performers out for lunch or dinner and personally thank them for their performance. Set a goal for the upcoming quarter or year. Set up an incentive program for your sales team and when they meet their goals, reward them. Remember, celebrate ALL VICTORIES!

What are your best selling products?

What do you sell the most of? What new products can you offer? Now is the time to plan your follow up calls with your current customers. What do they need, what do they want, and when can you set an appointment to make a personal contact?

What is in your future?

Have you set your goals? Have you debriefed your past performance? What has been working for you? What hasn't been working? What have you recently learned? Remember, debriefing is the answer to your future.

Have you set a financial goal?

Set a financial goal for your business this year. The most important part of setting a goal is writing it down and pinning it up where you will see it day in and day out. Break your financial goals down into months and monitor your results. Remember the effort you put into your business is the result you create. Make it incredible!

Chapter 29

Learning is a Skill

When we start a new job it takes 90 days, or about three months, to learn a job, but it takes one year to master it.

Just think back to your very first job. You were probably scared to death on day one but filled with excitement at the same time. During training you wondered how you were ever going to remember everything they taught you. You likely came home frustrated and felt overwhelmed. However, before you knew it, you had mastered your new job.

Learning comes in four stages. Awareness of these stages can help you improve your performance and results.

> **U.I. - Unconscious Incompetent** (not knowing that you don't know) - think back to when you wanted to drive a car. You had to take a written driver's test and then a series of in-car driving lessons. At first you probably didn't really know what to do but were not aware of this, you were just learning something new.
>
> **C.I. - Conscious Incompetence** (knowing that you don't know) - you take the lessons and are consciously aware that you don't know how to drive yet and need to learn how to.
>
> **C.C. - Conscious Competence** (knowing that you do know) - You now know how to drive the car. You have confidence in what you are doing.

U.C. - Unconscious Competence (not having to think about what you know) - you can drive the car, drink coffee and talk on the cell phone, not that this is a good practice — you don't even need to think about driving, you just know how to do it.

Competence comes from practice, correction, action, correction and more action.

In business, we cannot afford to operate from the U.I. level. Competence comes from practice, correction, action, correction and more action. We need to get to the level of U.C. so that we are competent in what we are doing.

Competent in your presentation skills
Competent in your closing skills
Competent in your customer service
Competent in your communication skills
Competent in your product

In sales, the mistake most people make is being sympathetic to our customers. If the customer falls into a hole, we crawl in with them to see if they are okay.

Become U.C. and empathize, not sympathize — with empathy you will pull your customer out of the hole.

When learning something new it requires you to PUSH....

P - PRACTICE
U - UNTIL
S - SOMETHING
H - HAPPENS

Never stop learning. Knowing how to learn is the key. Understanding the destination, Unconscious Competence, makes the journey easier. It's okay to not be excellent at something immediately. Persevere, PUSH forward, acquire competence and take ownership of the skill.

Chapter 30

What Not to Say in Sales

Have you ever been in a situation where you have heard the sales person say something that they shouldn't have?

Recently, I went out in search of a special evening dress for our 25th wedding anniversary. Often when purchasing evening gowns there is a no return or exchange policy that comes along with the sale. This is due to the fact that some women buy the dress, wear it and return the item the following day, which resulted in the high-end stores implementing this policy. I was so happy with the dress I purchased and, when I got home, I hung it on the door where it would sit until the special night. It was a backless dress with a V-front that had a metal clip on the dress. On our anniversary, I went to put the dress on but when the metal clip snapped in half, ruining the dress and making it unable to wear. The next week, I drove an hour back to the store to see the lady who sold it to me. She informed me, again, that they didn't take returns after which I explained my situation. She replied, "Well the dress wasn't broken when you left the store?" Now, I understand that the policy was "no returns", but there are times when you have to make exceptions. Customer service should always be a priority and when I told the lady I had driven an hour to bring it back she basically told me I should have called before coming to the store! They just lost a customer. Will I refer the store even though it has amazing dresses? No.

Never forget what built your business…your customers! Some of you may have built up your company from nothing. It was your idea, your business plan, your sweat and tears and your long hours. Remember this. In the end, without your customers your business would not survive. Treat your customers as you would like to be treated. Once you have the customers coming in, never stop improving what you do. What keeps someone coming back is the fact that you never stop ensuring the next time they come that their experience will be better than the last one. If your retention of customers is declining, it is time to stop and take a look at what you are doing. When we attract new customers, we sometimes don't notice the ones that are not coming back. Never stop thinking, looking or improving in your business.

Never forget what built your business... your customers!

One day I answered the phone and didn't recognize the voice of the person who was talking as though we were best friends. When he took a breath I said, "I'm sorry, I am not sure who this is." At that point he told me he was the car dealer that leased me my car three years ago and the lease was coming due. He wanted to know when I was coming in to pick out my next car. I asked him why he hadn't contacted me prior to two weeks before I was returning my car. He assumed he had a sale.

A few weeks later I was purchasing my new car and I was in the waiting area of the local BMW dealer. One of the salesmen came rushing up the stairs because he was late to see his client who was waiting reading the paper. The salesman shook his hand and said, "Sorry I am late, someone beat me to the elliptical trainer this morning and I had to wait for it." The customer had a confused look on his face as if to say, you chose to be late?

At a restaurant I asked the waitress if they could change the way the pasta was served and add vegetables. Her response was, "No, that is how we cook it!" and she said no more.

I was trying on a denim dress and it was made with spandex. On a personal note, spandex looks horrible on me! When I came out of the dressing room, the salesperson actually told me the dress looked great. It was way too big in the top and way too tight on the bottom. My girlfriend was with me and she just about burst out laughing. When I said to the sales person, "You don't really mean that do you?", she said, "Oh yes, I think it is fabulous on you and you should buy it." I proceeded back to the change room, gathered up my things and left the store.

Have you ever experienced service like this? Have you ever felt like you were intruding on the salesperson's time and energy? Have you ever felt like the salesperson was just trying to make the sale?

To be a good salesperson there are four qualities that are very important to have:

1. You must enjoy talking to people.
2. You talk to people even when you don't feel like talking to people.
3. You treat others as you would like to be treated.
4. You are honest and sincere to your customer.

Salespeople typically don't like other salespeople. Not necessarily because they are direct competition, but salespeople don't like being sold to. You can learn a lot about yourself when you are out buying something. Take note the next time you go out and are in a buying situation. How did the salesperson approach you? What did they say? Were they sincere or pushy? Did they try and close too quickly? Were they honest? What techniques did you like? What techniques didn't you like? Now, look at how you approach a sale the next time. Are you doing things that you didn't like when you were the buyer?

Chapter 31

Can You Really Make a Sale Anywhere?

Is there any place that you cannot make a sale? You can make a sale anywhere. It is a matter of how you carry yourself, what you say and how you treat people. I was recently on a business trip and after a long few days I decided to go to the spa. There was a steam room, so in I went. If you have never been in a steam room before, when you walk into full steam you cannot see a thing. You feel your way along the side until you reach the spot you want to sit. As the steam dissipated, I noticed that there was another woman sitting there. We started to chat and after she had told me about herself she asked what I did for a living. By the end of the conversation, she asked me to leave my contact details at the front desk and she would contact me. I had no business supplies or samples of my product. I had no literature to give her. All I had was my personality and passion for what I do. It is not about being pushy; it is about building rapport with people. When you have built rapport they will want to do business with you.

It is not about being pushy; it is about building rapport with people.

In sales, you need to take time out and acknowledge and appreciate yourself for everything you accomplish day to day. Many people don't appreciate the little things that they accomplish every day. I was out with a colleague the other day who spent the entire time telling me about all of the things that were going wrong in his business during the past month. He was solely focusing on what was going wrong. You need to focus on your successes as well as the things that didn't go well or else you will have a memory filled with upset and negative thoughts.

When you have a good sales call, write it down, what went well, what worked for you. I write in a journal daily and focus on the positive things that are happening. I also focus on three critical things I need to get done each day. At the end of the day, if I don't get them all done, I still celebrate what I did get done instead of focusing solely on what I didn't accomplish. By celebrating what I did accomplish, my energy and self-esteem are given a boost, which gives me what I need to go back out tomorrow. If you only remember your mistakes you won't be willing to go back out and take risks that can lead you to more successes.

Even when you are tired and can't be bothered, you need to keep your energy up. Your attitude is catching; make it a positive one whether you are the customer or the salesperson. You never know where or when you are going to meet your next customer.

Chapter 32

Attributes of a Successful Person in Sales

Circle the ones that apply to you right now.

1. They have very specific written goals. They stick to them, they review them on a regular basis and they have a burning desire to reach them. They hang them in their office or where they will see them every day.
2. They make a commitment to reaching their goals. When the goal is not achieved, they realize that they pushed further than they would have if they hadn't set the goal.
3. They learn from a top producer or mentor who leads by example. That way, they learn how a top producer achieves and then can follow in their footsteps.
4. They keep their office clutter-free. Clear the clutter from your office.
5. They keep accurate records of their business transactions daily so they don't get behind.
6. They are committed to the success of their team as well as their own personal success.
7. They have a professional voice message on their answering machine and respond to calls and emails within 24 hours.
8. They strive for excellent customer service. They treat others as they would like to be treated.
9. They are very informed on how to succeed in their business. They are constantly learning and updating their skills and

knowledge by making seminars, courses and meetings a priority.

10. They keep all appointments and agreements. They are always on time by being early.
11. They follow-up and follow through with prospects and customers.
12. They persevere with their commitment. They don't even use the word 'quit' in their vocabulary.
13. They are not discouraged by small problems or inconveniences.
14. They do not talk negatively about other people or companies who may be their competitors.
15. They are serious about their business. They treat it as a business, not a hobby.
16. They work on their own personal development by reading books, listening to audios, going to seminars.
17. They are helpful to others in their business even if they have nothing to gain by sharing. People helping people.
18. They are professional in their appearance and go dressed for business. Ask yourself, would you want to deal with you? In the blink of an eye a first impression is made.
19. They are professional about the appearance of the products they sell. No tattered boxes, etc.
20. They believe in the products they sell and learn about them so they can best serve their customers.
21. They handle customer complaints in a timely and cheerful manner.
22. They are quick to praise and recognize the achievements of their team.
23. They work their business on a daily basis. Ten calls a day will build their business.
24. They are happy for the success of their team and they strive to constantly encourage growth of co-workers and the company as a whole.
25. They take responsibility for their own actions, failures and successes.
26. They put out great effort and expect great results.
27. They associate only with like-minded people who are

positive.

28. They are patient and they know that their success is on the way.
29. They pass on information to their team in a timely fashion.
30. They never complain, especially at business meetings and events.
31. They believe in their company and product.
32. They just work hard.
33. They never depend on spill-over to be successful. They depend on themselves.
34. They are willing to invest in their business to make it successful, such as investing in personal and professional development tools, brochures, advertising, flyers, incentive gifts, training, etc.
35. They never take 'NO' personally. To them 'NO' only means not now and gets them closer to a 'YES.'
36. They are flexible and cope with changes in a positive manner.
37. They attend all company functions and invest in themselves.
38. They are not influenced by negative comments by their family members, relatives or friends.
39. They spend time talking to prospects.
40. They are patient with learning their business and realize that it takes time to build it at first.
41. They plan to succeed; no other alternative is given any thought.
42. They do not gossip or lay blame. They do not listen to rumors and deal direct with people.
43. They never give excuses.
44. They are ready and willing to learn.
45. They keep up with the latest information and what is new in their industry.
46. They stay physically fit and full of energy.
47. They always strive to do their best.
48. They sell themselves on themselves - the biggest sale of all.
49. They believe that sales bring income.
50. They truly believe that selling requires energy!

Refer back to the list and unlock the key to attributes that can bring success to your business. Now that you are aware of these attributes, you can use them to improve your skill set. Remember, it's about practice, correction and action!

Use this list to improve your skill set.

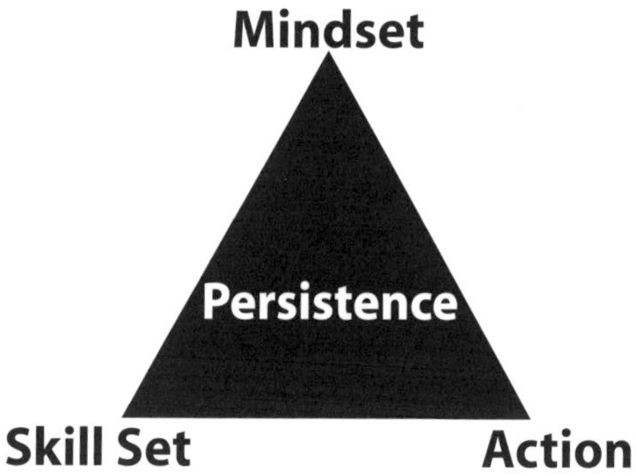
Mindset
Persistence
Skill Set
Action

PART 3
Action

Chapter 33

Action Introduction

"It is time for us all to stand and cheer for the doer, the achiever — the one who recognizes the challenge and does something about it."
Vincent Lombardi

You can think and learn all you want but until you act, nothing changes. Have you ever had great intentions? You know what I mean. You get up and tell yourself that today you are going to get so much accomplished and then the phone rings and your friend is asking you out for lunch. You are then torn between going out for lunch or working. As a self-employed businesswoman, sometimes going for lunch gets the better of me. Friends and family sometimes don't get it, that when I am at home I am indeed working. They think that you can come and go as you please and that you can stop or start working on a dime. That may be true, but the key to success is the ACTION we take.

When I was facilitating a conference call for our direct sales team, I said to them, "You can think all day long of the business you want, but until you pick up that phone and get working your business, you will still be in the same spot you are in right now." It isn't easy picking up the phone or going out and hitting the streets, but when you do, your actions will turn into income.

Confidence is powerful energy.

Taking ACTION requires confidence. Confidence is powerful energy. Everyone has some form confidence. We are confident our feet will walk one in front of the other to get us across the room. We are confident when we sit down in a chair that it will hold us. My daughter jumped out of a plane and she was confident that her parachute would open. We are confident that the wheels will stay on our car when we get into it and drive along the highway. If you are confident in your business, or about your product or service, it will show up as powerful energy. If our mind is full of doubt, our doubt will turn into fear and it will stop action. Fear turns into anxiety. Confidence comes from practicing what we need to practice. Knowing our product or service inside out and then having a passion to go out and create business. That is what keeps developing your self confidence.

With Action, there are steps that we can take:

1. Coming up with an idea or thought.
2. Having the will to take that thought or idea into action.
3. Imagine who you will present it to.
4. Perceiving how the deal will close.
5. Reasoning why you want the sale.

Really, what are you taking action for? If you look at your life right now, is it what you want? If the answer is "no", then action is needed to make a change. You have the ability to create what ever you want. You have the ability to take action to get what you want and create the income you want. If you ask successful people what they are doing to get where they are, many of them will tell you that they have multiple streams of income. They take action in different areas.

As an example, my husband and I decided to buy a home that needed to be renovated and sold it for an additional stream of income. Now, this house was standing, but the inside was a disaster. You could hardly breathe when you walked in the front door. Everything about the house was disgusting. I could go into detail but you might get sick hearing about it. The day we started working in the house was the day after the Citizen of the Year Award dinner that I was honored at. Our insurance man was coming over to take photos of this house so we would be insured. When he arrived, I was taking wallpaper off the walls in the living room and the nicotine was running down the walls. I had a mask on and gloves up to my elbows. He looked at me and said "Lori; Citizen of the Year one day and look at you now." He had the look on his face like, what are you doing this for, you have a successful business? My husband actually wanted to pull our insurance from their company for his smart remark. My dad came to see the house too. He walked in and walked right out shaking his head, never coming back. Being in the fashion business, I am always dressed up and put together, so this was a total reversal for me. I found myself going into the coffee shop covered with paint, fitting right in with all the construction workers who were on their break.

The basement of this house had a section where it was a dirt floor and needed to be covered with cement. They were re-doing the sidewalks on the street so I decided to take action and go and ask the cement truck driver what kind of cement I would need to fill in the space. He stopped the truck and followed me to the house and came downstairs. He then told me that I could use the same cement that he used and at the end of the day he would leave a pile at the end of the driveway for me. I thanked him for being so kind and I then asked, "How am I supposed to get the cement from the end of the driveway to the basement?" He smiled and said, "We will be by at 4:30." When the work men arrived there were four of them all carrying pails of cement. Within 15 minutes they had poured the cement for me, and then the cement finisher evened it all out and it was done. I offered to go and get them coffee but they politely declined. When they left, I celebrated the victory! Later that night, my husband came by and I told him to go and look downstairs. He came back upstairs and said, "How did you get that done?" When I told him I just went out and asked the cement truck driver he laughed and said, "Way to go!"

After the house was completely gutted and put back together, my niece came over one day to pick me up. She asked if she could come in and see the house. She loved the house. She was getting married soon and told me that it would be perfect for them, she was interested in buying it. She didn't see the "before" and loved the new almost-finished home. When my dad found out that she wanted to make an offer he could not believe it. In the end, I didn't want her to buy the home as doing business with family previously did not work out. My niece understood and I thanked her for the encouragement. The house was on the market for two days and we had worked on it for two and a half months. Our profit on the sale after expenses was $30,000. When we called the insurance company to take the insurance off, he came by the house and was absolutely amazed that it was the same place and I couldn't help myself but to tell him what the profit was. My husband and I had never been handy and we always hired people to do various jobs around our house. Completing this house was a huge accomplishment. We learned how to do things we never dreamed we'd be doing. I spent a lot of time at Home Depot being taught different techniques. I actually had fun learning. We have now taken action and fixed four homes profiting over $120,000.00. Not bad for approximately nine months of side jobs. When we call the insurance man now, he is more than happy to get us the best quotes on the market because he knows we mean business.

Experience is what you get when you don't get what you want.

In the journey of my business life, if I had listened to most people, I would not be doing what I am doing today. If you want something, just take action. If it doesn't work out, experience is what you get when you don't get what you want. So you just chock it up to experience, learn the lesson and try again.

Let's look at the previous list of steps and how they change when action is taken:

1. Coming up with an idea or thought — *buy a house to fix up and re-sell.*
2. Having the will to take that thought or idea into action — *go to the bank and get the money to buy the house, then plan the renovations.*
3. Imagine who you will present it to — *seeing the house completely renovated and a new family moving in happy with their purchase.*
4. Perceiving how the deal will close — *we visualized fast and making a profit.*
5. Reasoning why you want the sale — *an additional income stream.*

The reason we wanted the sale was to have an additional income stream that would pay for our daughter's university education. She was in a four-year program, which is why we did four homes. We used to call the houses University Year 1, University Year 2 — you get the picture. She graduated with an Honors Bachelor of Science degree and the profit from the houses paid her way. If you have a reason, it really does help you to take the action required to make it a reality. We are proud to say she finished debt free and as a family we have worked on the houses to allow this to happen. We have now taught our kids that you can make money by taking action and you never know when the door of opportunity will open.

Give thought, create the mind set, learn the skills and take action!

When the power of intention is so strong and you compress the space of time you take to start or complete something, you will see incredible results. If you want something, go after it NOW, don't wait, take action. It is a three step process. You have given thought and created a mind set, you learn the skills and you take action. Before you know it you will have results. And to take it a step further, the results will be able to pay for your dreams.

Chapter 34

Have a Plan of Action

Why not work backwards. Visualize yourself already achieving what you want and then work backwards to achieve it. The foundation of all success is knowing first what you want to achieve.

For instance, when I go out to do product shows for my direct sales business, I always state what I want to achieve before I drive out of the driveway. I want an $800 show with 2 bookings. I think of what I can do for my hostess to allow her to have a sensational night and how I am going to make the customers feel when they arrive. Ninety-nine percent of the time I am right with my projections.

Visualize where you want to be 12 months from now and work backwards. What do you want to be doing or earning 10 months from now, 8 months from now and so on? Work backwards until you get to the actions that can support your vision. What action can you take today to make it happen? The biggest mistakc I have made in my businesses is failing to see the vision.

In business, I have seen so many deals go bust because the salesperson was too anxious, thinking of the transaction to benefit themselves rather than benefiting the other person. Make a conscious decision to focus your action on the other person, rather than yourself, and you will see your sales soar.

As you begin to take action towards the fulfillment of your goals and dreams, you must realize that not every action will be perfect. Not every action will produce the results that you want. Not every action will work. Correct fast and continue taking action. Keep in motion. An object in motion tends to stay in motion. The faster you make mistakes and correct, the stronger your business will be.

The faster you make mistakes and correct, the stronger your business will be.

If you can adopt the attitude of persistence, then you can be free to take action. Debrief the results you get and adjust your next actions based on the feedback you receive. It's action, feedback, adjustment and action once again.

No plan of action equals no action. If you aren't getting what you want in business, look at the volume of activity going on.

Chapter 35

Are You Really Giving Your Best?

In sales and in life you need to do your best. By not doing your best, you don't produce the desired results. Without results, you don't earn an income. Without an income, you can't live to the standards that you want. Without giving your best, you may not reach your goals and dreams.

So what is your best?

I was at a seminar in a room of 125 people and the energy was very low at the outset. As the four days went on, the momentum grew, and by the last day when a car was given away, we could have blown the roof off the building. Being at a business conference like this, you have two choices. You can get involved and network or you can sit back and watch everyone else do it.

I watched the pattern of people. When I saw them getting tired and low on energy, the first place they went was for coffee and energy drinks. These drinks are just quick fixes to give us that burst we need. But in order to be our best we need to fuel our bodies with a different kind of energy. Sometimes the coffee and energy drinks can zap us of our energy more than we actually know. What are you doing in your business/life to fuel yourself with different energy that can increase your production and success?

When you go to work do you give your best? Do you give more than your best? Think back to the last 48 hours and do an analysis of this time period. Did you give your best?

Today, in business and in life many people are overworked, stressed and tired. We want to do so much and accomplish so much to be our best but we run out of steam.

The only thing that is holding any of us back is about six inches — the space between your left and right ear. It's that inner voice inside our head — period! We say, "I'm so tired," "I don't have energy," "I can't get anything done," "I don't feel like doing that," and so on. We need to stop ourselves and fill up with good energy that lasts. I have found that just 30 minutes of exercise can fuel me for the entire day. When I am tired and I truly look at what I am eating and doing, it is quite clear that it was self inflicted. I am eating sweets, drinking lattés and not working out. My travel schedule isn't the best for keeping on track but I can make excuses all day long. The only person who can keep me on track, is me! Right after that conference, I made the point to work out daily, refrain from eating junk and drinking coffee. I drank 6-8 glasses of water and got more sleep. I was energized. I was then operating at my "best" level.

When people talk negatively to me I stay away from them. To be quite blunt, my circle of friends have changed since I have been traveling because the ones who say, "Oh you are going away again?" I don't call anymore. I need to move forward and hang out with like-minded people. Don't get me wrong, I still love my friends but they don't see the vision that I do and don't have the same mission. They can zap me of my energy. It isn't right or wrong, it just is. Some people would not want to travel but I love it so it works for me.

It takes practice to stay positive and be at your best.

By managing the inner voice inside our head, we can actually train ourselves to be more positive. It has reduced my stress and my mind is not as cluttered. When my mind starts wandering or I start doubting myself I just say, "Knock it off Lori." It really helps. We can be our own worst enemies. It becomes a habit to manage that inner voice inside my head and it also takes practice to stay positive and be my best.

One of my favorite things to do is go for a walk first thing in the morning or late at night. I was in an accident in 1992 when the overhead compartment in the plane opened and a large metal case fell out and hit me on the head. I had five years of intensive therapy. My doctor wanted me to give up my business and do nothing, so I could heal. I asked him, "If this had happened to you, would you give up your practice?" He thought I had a nice little sales business when in fact I was earning the same income that he was. I was in a peak period and my husband just started his own business, so giving up my career was out of the question. I then needed to find a doctor who would work with me and understand that I wasn't willing to give into the pain and quit.

In the hospital pain program that I was enrolled in, they taught us to walk and be thankful. It is a great way to start the day…so when I walk I am always aware of what is around me. Those who walk with me have learned this technique too. I notice the flowers, the sunrise or sunset, the dogs that are always happy to be with their owners, the smell of the seasons for example. Walking and being thankful gives me a double zap of energy and if I go at the end of the day it finishes the day off positively. It really works and so the one thing I got from that terrible accident was that I learned to be thankful on a daily basis. Take some time today to go for a walk outside, winter or summer, and look around you. Take time to smell the roses if they are in season or look at the beauty of the snow on the ground. Really look at what is around you, excite your senses and be thankful.

During a trip to South Africa, I was making a sale. It is truly amazing that, no matter where you are in the world, a sale is a sale. I found making a sale there just as easy as making one here. All I had to do was ask. On the other side of the world they buy and sell just like we do. On the street corners where newspapers are sold I noticed that the local paper was trying to change the way the community sees paper sellers. Most people just see them as beggars — but the Homeless Paper saw them as entrepreneurs who have gotten out of a homeless situation by selling papers. I went to speak at their launch and was so inspired. I bought papers while there and watched their selling style. Those who sold a paper and didn't offer change bothered the purchasing drivers. However the ones with positive energy who gave change were frequently told to keep it. The selling styles were similar, but some had more energy than others and they were the ones making a lot of sales. A few dragged themselves to the cars while others bounced towards their customers with big smiles on their face when asking for the sale. Remember, in a selling situation when there are two people, the person with the highest energy and excitement will always get the sale, no matter where you are.

When you commit to the highest advantage of others... the universe will always provide.

Here is something to think about: when you commit yourself to the highest advantage of others...the universe will always provide.

Chapter 36

Do You Watch Things Happen?

When I left full-time employment to pursue my own business, only one person was supportive and that was my husband. I initially received so many negative comments , like, "What if it doesn't work?" The people who told me that I would not succeed 20 years ago try and take credit for my success today by saying that it was a great idea. They now say that I was lucky to have left that job and that I have so much more flexibility owning my own business.

Do you watch things happen, make things happen or wonder what happened?

In sales, you will fall into one of the three categories above. You can lead, follow or get out of the way. Do you want to be a passenger or a member of the crew?

> **You can lead, follow, or get out of the way.**

If you don't believe in yourself or your product, no matter how easy a sale it is, you will not get the results you are after — it will show. You may find yourself holding back from attempting to sell your product because you are not confident.

Do you have a mentor that has believed in you and encouraged you to reach your goals, helped you through difficult times or taught you something and made you feel like you could achieve anything? I have had a few mentors in my life and it is those people who have made me push harder because they believed in me. Some of my mentors have been professionals but some have been ordinary people who just flat out cared about me. Who have you been a mentor to? Who have you made feel special and appreciated?

When you feel appreciated, you will go the extra mile no matter what the cost or time involved.

When my kids were young, I felt as though I was always being negative with them … "No, don't do this," "Don't do that," "Stop this," "Stop that." I came up with a system that worked for me in many areas of my life and in business and I challenge you to do the same.

Go and find 10 pennies right now. Put them in your right pocket. Each day, your goal is to empty the pennies from your right pocket to your left pocket and show appreciation to people. Each time you show appreciation to someone, move one penny to your left pocket. When I did this with my kids, I used the pennies to give praise to them. In a few short days, it was miraculous what a difference it made around our home.

I then used the pennies to praise my husband and show appreciation for him.

Next, I used it when leading my team at meetings by encouraging people and raising them up to be who they really can be. Their sales soared.

The power of appreciation is very strong. Sometimes we just need to focus on acknowledging and appreciating the people in our life.

You can use the 10 pennies for how many "cold calls" you want to do or how many new clients you want to obtain or how many past clients you want to call. How many sales do you want to have?

The feeling of accomplishment when the pennies are all in the other pocket is a reason to celebrate the win. I tried hard not to end the day unless my pennies were switched over.

When I did this for a month it became an unconscious habit for me. My business increased, my confidence increased and my relationships had a whole new meaning. I then became a mentor to many people.

Chapter 37

Have You Ever Gotten Detoured?

On my way to a meeting, there was a bad accident on the highway and the roads were closed. We were detoured off the highway by the police and I didn't know where I was going. The accident delayed me and I was late, which was against my number one rule in business — do not be late for an appointment! Luckily I had my cell phone with me so I called to let them know what was happening. As I drove along the detour, my car went into a big pothole. The next thing I knew I had a flat tire. Frustrated, I pulled over and got out of my car in my high heels and business suit. I have never changed a tire and didn't have the first clue how to do it....so I guess that was something I needed to learn. I had roadside assistance service so I immediately called them and I was informed it would be 45 minutes before they could get there.

> **Do not be late for an appointment.**

Sales are like a detour in the road. Sometimes we know where our next sale is coming from and sometimes we don't have a clue. We get complacent, lazy and sometimes just down-right unfocused. We get a personal flat tire. Sometimes we just need to be blown up and other times we need to make a change. In your business are you taking the road less traveled or the route you know? Sometimes we drive to our destination and we don't even remember how we got there. In sales, we get so accustomed to making the sale that we don't appreciate the sale or how we got it. Do we get stagnant when we have a repeat customer or do we value their business like it was the first sale we made?

Every journey begins with a road map and a vision to go somewhere and do something. If you have the desire and vision then you also have the power to make it happen. To see the road ahead, you have to have desire. After all, how can we drive somewhere if we don't know where we are going? Ask yourself these important questions as you drive down the highway of life:

- What is my vision for my business?
- What direction do I want to go in?
- Do I know how to get there?

When you are thinking about your vision and what your goals are, sometimes it is better to just go and do it. If you think about it too much you may be wasting valuable time. I have seen it over and over again when people spend too much time thinking about what they want to do rather than actually going out and doing it. Having a vision for your future helps you get going in the right direction. It gives you something to drive towards and gives you tools to help you overcome the obstacles that might come your way.

Write down what you want to accomplish and plan your route the night before. That way when you get up in the morning you will have a clear vision for your day.

During the journey of sales, you will be hit with roadblocks and potholes from time to time and you may need to get your tire changed. These challenges may cause us to stop, turn around and give up. If you keep your eyes focused on the road ahead and keep your vision in mind, you will move past these road blocks and take a detour that will get you to your destination.

For me, that day on the highway — life just happened. There was nothing I could do about the detour signs and the change of route. I had to be patient. Thankfully my customer was patient also and the sale was closed. It ended up being a successful ride in the end, just a little bumpy. You see, it's not what happens to you, but how you choose to handle it, that determines the outcome.

It's not what happens to you, but how you choose to handle it...

Here's my tip. Write down what you want to accomplish each day. Do the things you don't want to do first, and you will get them over with. Then the rest of the day will be yours to do what you really want to do.

Chapter 38

Discipline, Practice and Accountability

- Are you hitting your sales target or the bull's-eye?
- Are you taking the short cut or the scenic route?
- What are you reaching for?
- What do you want to establish?
- Are you content where your business is?
- Do you want more than you experienced last week, last month or last year?
- Do you want to be more successful in your business?
- Do you read these types of books to be motivated?
- Do you take action?

Close your eyes for a moment and imagine yourself standing at a river bank. The water is flowing by splashing against the rocks that line the river. All of a sudden you notice that there is money floating in the water, lots of money. Would you jump in and grab all of the money or would you stand on the edge of the river and watch it float by?

Sales can be thought of as the riverbank and we have two choices; we can jump in or just stand there waiting for things to happen. We can call on a new client or wait for a new client to call us. What is your vision for your business?

"Is there anything worse than being blind?
Yes, a man with sight and no vision."
Helen Keller.

No vision = no action
No action = no sales
No sales = no income
No income = no business

Do you have customers you have been meaning to call on? What is holding you back from just going out and doing it?

If you had 20 clams on a plate and I told you one clam housed the most magnificent pearl, would you open just one clam to find the pearl? Would you give up and stop searching? No, I bet you would persist until you found the beautiful pearl! The same is true in sales; we need to keep on persisting until we get the close.

- Do you have a bad attitude?
- Do you have enthusiasm and a passion for what you are doing?
- Do you take responsibility for yourself or blame others?
- Do you set goals regularly?
- Are you self disciplined and committed?
- Do you recognize success as hard work?
- Do you believe in yourself and your business?

In 2002 I ran the New York City Marathon. Preparing for the race took training, endurance and proper equipment. A marathon is 26.2 miles or 42 kilometers. The first 10 kilometers you are running, talking to other runners, excited and pumped. At the 15km mark you start to feel pain both physically and mentally. At 18km you start getting physically numb and the mental pain really kicks in. The inner voice inside my head started to tell me that I was too old for this and that I made a stupid decision by choosing to run the race.

A simple strategy helped me overcome that inner voice and endure the physical pain. It was easy; “Left foot, right foot, left foot, right foot.” Once I crossed the finish line I was a legend in my own mind. I instantly forgot about the pain and suffering I just endured. I caught myself then saying, “Wow this was fantastic. Let's do it again.” “I knew I could do it, this was a great idea.” The physical pain lasted about five days after the marathon and it was a pain of accomplishment. Running a business is like running a marathon — you are in for the long haul. Some selling is like going to the 10 kilometer mark where you are pumped and close quickly, with the cash in hand. Some are more draining both mentally and physically. Some selling cycles take a long time and it is like running a marathon until you complete the cycle.

In your business, what is your pain? If you don't have a system in place, that could be your pain. If you don't have a plan and half your day is wasted figuring out what you are going to do next, that could be the pain. What is your system? Do you have an accounting system, a selling system, a closing system, a marketing system — to name a few? The strategy is simple, “Left foot, right foot.” It is one step at a time.

Discipline

What are you doing to discipline yourself in your business? What increases do you want to see and how are you going to get there? Do you have a plan of action? To create a plan of action, here is what I recommend: every night before you retire, debrief your day. We've covered this several times already, but it's critical… What worked? What didn't work? What did you learn? What did you learn about yourself? Then plan for tomorrow. What can you improve on? Who are you going to call on? Make your list the night before so your next day is a productive one.

Practice

Are you practicing how to handle the questions and objections you typically get from your customers? The key to handling objections is acknowledging the objection and asking a question. Practice this until you are a master at handling objections. For example, your customer says, "Your price is too expensive." You reply: "Thank you. Why do you feel it is too expensive?" or "Thank you. Expensive compared to what?" Here is another, "Why should I consider doing business with you?" You reply: "That's a good question. Who do you currently do business with?"

There are many things to practice in order to be successful in sales. Practicing your presentation skills is another key element. Practice, debrief, correct and practice again…

Accountability

Who or what are you accountable to? Is it your boss, yourself, your family, your statistics? If the answer is to nobody, find someone who will hold you accountable. Have your mentor or coach help you get to the next level in your business. Give them the permission to be blunt and honest. A mentor or coach will have your best interest at heart.

Assign a consequence if you do not accomplish what you set out to do.

Another successful strategy for accountability is to assign a consequence if you do not accomplish what you set out to do. If you are accountable to someone and your word is your worth, then you may need a consequence that hurts you enough to not want to miss the goal again. Sometimes something as simple as denying a pleasure, food, TV or a movie, may be enough to cause you to work harder to get what you are after. Consequences are a great way to utilize accountability effectively.

Chapter 39

Getting Your Business off the Ground

I love being on an airplane, especially at night when you can look down and see the cities all lit up.

As I glance at the lights, I visualize the opportunity that is out there for us. All we have to do is go after it. We can compare success to an airplane; most of our energy is spent getting off the ground. How do we get our sales to soar? What do we need to do, both personally and business-wise, to make it happen? The first thing we have to do is buckle our seat belts and get ready for the ride. Next, we have to set our course and make sure that we stay on course. Have you seen the new GPS systems in cars today? They are fantastic — if you take a wrong turn, the car actually tells you that you are going the wrong way and it redirects your route so you can get back on track. Now, wouldn't that be amazing in business if, every time we got off track, someone talked to us and told us we were off course. In selling, you have to be good at asking questions and finding out what your customer wants and needs. You also have to listen and be good at knowing what to say after your prospect answers your questions. If your presentation is practiced and polished you will be more prepared to close the deal. As we said earlier, practice, practice, practice!

Not too long ago I was in Phoenix and I climbed Squaw Peak. I thought I was in good shape and I climbed up with a very good athlete. Trying to pretend that I was not exhausted, I started to slow down. My breathing got heavy and it was 100 degrees, making the rock very hot. I couldn't hold on to the rock because of the heat. I was trying not to look down as we went up. Once we got to the top, the view was spectacular. As it began to get dark, we sat on the rock and looked out over Phoenix. As I sat there, I was in awe and kept telling myself that there is more opportunity for each and every one of us if we stop and look ahead and go for it. I have seen it many times in my direct selling business where people don't want to invite others to join them in business because they want to keep the business for themselves. They think that inviting their friends and family into the business will take sales away from them. However, if we duplicate, there is always enough to go around and sales actually multiply. You have to see the bigger picture.

Sales have a precession effect. This means, by definition, the act or state of preceding. Precession is the effect of a body in motion on another body in motion. When we drop a stone into a pond, we create ripples — the precession effect of the stone affecting the water.

The bee goes in search of food, nectar. However, this process has been set up by nature so that the bee also acts as a pollinator at the same time. What if the bee decides to help ants dig into the ground to make their home? Honey production would stop. Flowers wouldn't get pollinated. The world would suffer.

So what happens if you commit yourself to the precession effect of what you do (pollination), rather than honey creation (making money)? Nature will reward us with more "honey" than we could have imagined creating by ourselves. Your significance may forever be obscure to you. What's important is that you commit yourself to the advantage of others. Precession is predicated upon being in motion.

Do you have the courage to focus on the precession of your business and trust that the money will flow? Think about the precession effect that you can have on your business if you open the door of opportunity. Create a ripple effect in your business.

Chapter 40

If You are Going to Fall, Fall Forward

In autumn each year, the leaves fall off the trees. If you watch the leaves, some fall forward and some fall backwards. In business, we can fall forward or we can fall backwards.

Have you ever made a sales call, gotten back in your car and wondered what went wrong? Let me tell you about Walter, a man who I have been training. He took the challenge of making 100 cold calls in a two day period. He had never made cold calls before and when he went through the process, he not only learned a lot about the business owners that he called on, but he learned a lot about himself.

One call that Walter went on was with a business owner who was downright rude. The man crumpled up Walter's business card and threw it back at him. Walter had decided to take his nine-year-old son on this call to show him first hand what his challenge was. When they got back in the car, Walter felt deflated. He looked at his son and said, “If I can't go back in there and deal with how I was treated, I might as well get out of this business.” So out of the car he went and marched right back in to see the business owner again. He asked for an explanation as to why he got blown off and treated so rudely. The business owner told him that he used to be a combat officer and he could make anyone, anywhere, admit to a crime even if they didn't do it. He said, “Today I just felt like being like that with you.” Well, Walter took a deep breath and asked him if they could start over. The business owner was so impressed he had come back, that he decided to listen to what Walter had to say. After his sales pitch, he handed the business owner another card after which he said, "Well, I'm going to keep this card! I know I will be contacting you in the future to do business together."

Just before Walter had called to give me his stats, I was reading the book Rich Dad Poor Dad, by Robert Kiyosaki, for the fifth time. I was on page 33 when Walter called. This is what the page said:

> *Most of the time, life does not talk to you. It just sort of pushes you around. Each push is life saying, "Wake up. There's something I want you to learn."*
>
> *"If you learn life's lessons, you will do well. If not, life will just continue to push you around. People do two things. Some just let life push them around. Others get angry and push back. But they push back against their boss, or their job, or their husband or wife. They do not know it's life that's pushing."*
>
> *Life pushes all of us around. Some give up. Others fight. A few learn the lesson and move on. They welcome life pushing them around. To these few people, it means they need and want to learn something. They learn and move on. Most quit, and a few like you fight."*
>
> *Rich dad continued. "Or if you're the kind of person who has no guts, you just give up every time life pushes you. If you're that kind of person, you'll live all your life playing it safe, doing the right things, saving yourself for some event that never happens. Then you die a boring old man. You'll have lots of friends who really like you because you were such a nice hard-working guy. You spent a life playing it safe, doing the right things. But the truth is, you let life push you into submission. Deep down you were terrified of taking risks. You really wanted to win, but the fear of losing was greater*

than the excitement of winning. Deep inside, you and only you will know you didn't go for it.

This was exactly where Walter was that day. During this experience he made the decision that he was not going to give up. He needed to learn a lesson from this and decided to push back. He pushed back and was able to move on. He was not going to quit. When I shared with Walter what I was reading at that moment, he was elated. He got his 100 calls in and completed the task. He said he learned so much about himself and that making those calls is all about building rapport within the community. He learned that it wasn't really a big deal.

Are you ready to change your life today? Here's your challenge. Go out and make 100 calls in two days. Meet people you don't know. Go in and find out a little bit about their business and tell them a little bit about yours. You will learn a lot, just as Walter did — he fell forward. You will generate new business, start some new relationships and end up with more new customers. Learn to take "no" professionally, not personally. Go for it!

Learn to take "no" professionally, not personally.

I heard this cute story a long time ago:

> Lucy and Charlie Brown were on a cruise ship. They were out on the front deck of the ship. Lucy said, "Charlie Brown today a lot of people will come out here to the front deck of the ship and they will get their chairs and they will put them out here. They are facing forward. There are people who want to see where they are going and they will sit here all day just to see where they are going."
>
> Then she took Charlie Brown to the back of the ship and she said, "Now Charlie there are some people who are going to sit at the back of the ship. They want to sit here all day because they want to see where they have been."

> Then she looked at Charlie Brown and in the typical Lucy fashion and said to him, “The question I have for you is, where are you going to put your deck chair?”
>
> Charlie Brown replied, “I have no idea Lucy, I can't even find my deck chair!”

There are some people who face forward and some who look back, and some who can't even find their chair. Which way are you facing?

Chapter 41

If You KNEW You Could Not Fail... What Would You Do?

When I was speaking in Edmonton, Alberta I wanted to be able to start my talk by building rapport with those in attendance. You know what I mean, go into their world first. I headed to the West Edmonton Mall, one of the world's largest malls. They have an amusement park right in the mall and that is where I headed. I had heard of a ride called the Mind Bender, a very high roller coaster. I bought a ticket and onto the ride I went. I was the only passenger. When I got to the top, my heart was pounding. At the top, I felt like I was momentarily suspended in mid-air before I went shooting straight down towards the ground. I started screaming and my knuckles were white by the time the ride had stopped. When I was speaking the next day, I asked the audience of 500 how many of them had gone on this ride and only a few people put their hands up. I went up to a man who had his hand up and asked him what his impression was at the first drop. He let out a blood curdling scream and the audience went wild. That was the ice breaker for my talk.

I am terrified of roller coasters. Taking the leap of faith to conquer my fear was scary; however, I just had to do it. Have you ever felt this way in sales? You just knew you could not fail but then something stopped you?

During a two day event in South Africa, one of the participants had just started a new job. After the program, he went back to work with a renewed enthusiasm and was so excited. He was given a budget to hit by the year end and, with his transformed attitude he exceeded his quota in one day! His attitude was that he knew he could not fail. As a matter of fact, he then had the company re-set his expectations and the company's as well. They were expecting far less than they could get.

Imagine if you could just go out and ask for whatever you wanted. Let's say your product is worth $500. What if you could ask five times the price? What would that voice inside your head be saying? Asking for what you are worth…

How has this month been so far? Have you been closing left and right and following up on all of your leads and prospects? Maybe your month isn't going the way you had hoped. Have you put in the effort you thought you would or have you been coasting? Maybe you are stopping your day at 3 o'clock instead of 5 o'clock and you are not working that hard. Maybe you are feeling a little un-motivated.

Our deepest fear is
not that we are inadequate.
Our deepest fear is
that we are powerful beyond measure.
It is our light, not our darkness,
that most frightens us.
We ask ourselves,
Who am I to be brilliant, gorgeous,
talented and fabulous?
Actually who are you not to be?
You are a child of God.
Your playing small doesn't serve the world.
There's nothing enlightened about
shrinking so that other people

won't feel insecure around you.
We were born to manifest
the glory of God that is within us.
It is not just in some of us; It's in everyone.
And as we let our own light shine,
we unconsciously give other people
permission to do the same.
As we are liberated from our own fear,
our presence automatically liberates others.

Nelson Mandela (1994)

Is a "no" a failure? "No" is just "no" — don't get hung up on it. It's part of the process. If you knew you could not fail, what would you do? Probably a lot more than what you are currently doing. Act as if… Dare to be great, you are capable of so much more and you deserve it!

Chapter 42

Being Consistent

What does being consistent really mean?

I believe it is a part of our human nature. We have a strong desire to be consistent in our lives. When we open our eyes in the morning, we want to find the floor under our feet, the sun above our heads and coffee or tea in our cups. We want our cars to start so we can get to work and we want our days to be normal. We expect consistency in a physical state but we also want it in a mental state. If we had jobs and families yesterday, we expect to find them in the same order today. Consistency holds everything together. To me, it is the cement that holds life together. All in all, people expect consistency.

Being inconsistent causes confusion and interruption in our lives. We then try to figure out what went wrong or what we missed. Inconsistency causes feelings of distress, anxiety and an uncomfortableness for many. In business, everything goes well when I follow a system, but goes awry when I try to do it on my own whim.

Being inconsistent causes confusion and interruptions in our lives.

When life gets inconsistent, we want to make changes to get things back to a consistent state. We sometimes need to change our expectations of a situation or evaluate the event differently.

Why is it that we procrastinate on daily tasks? Why is it so hard to stay focused and be organized? When we are consistent, it helps us to have quality time both in business and at home. When we are not consistent in what we do, nothing seems to run smoothly. Take a few minutes to answer these questions:

- What keeps you up at night? Is it money issues, fear of rejection or fear of closing a sale?

- What has been your biggest success to date in your business?

- How can you set yourself up to be a winner in sales? What changes do you need to make?

- Are you focusing on things that will put $ in the bank or are you spending a lot of time spinning your wheels?

What seeds are you consistently planting in your business to create growth? Take the daisy flower. You can throw its seeds anywhere and the flowers will grow stronger every year. Sales is like planting seeds. Have you made a sale and then not followed through to have a repeat customer? It is important to nurture your customer and make the relationship stronger. If you want to be a leader in your business, consider this list of things to refrain from saying:

- "I didn't have time"
- "I didn't think about asking that"
- "They didn't get back to me"
- "I thought someone else was taking care of that"
- "No one told me that"

In business we can choose to lead the way or follow. I just read a fascinating article about the "bell cow." This cow is the one that leads the other cows back to the barn at milking time. The farmer recognizes this cow as a leader and puts a bell around its neck which helps the other cows learn and follow it. Are you like the bell cow that wants to step up and lead or are you like the cows in the herd that will just follow?

Be consistent in everything you do and don't get caught up in day-to-day time wasters. Don't be afraid to delegate and stop spreading yourself so thin. It is common for us to refrain from saying "no" but it is okay to do so. Screen your calls so your phone is not permanently attached to your head. Take time away from the computer and email. And when you are procrastinating, do what you don't want to do first to get the ball rolling.

Don't get caught up in day-to-day time wasters.

Don't let obstacles get you down. Beethoven's teacher called him hopeless. She didn't like the way he handled the violin or that he preferred to play his own compositions. Walt Disney was fired by a newspaper for lacking ideas. He also went bankrupt before he built Disneyland. Obstacles will cross our path many times during our life; we just have to go around them or through them.

The single greatest key to success in sales is the ability to be consistent in your goals, presentation, communication and in your day-to-day activities.

As Winston Churchill said, in the face of adversity, "Never, never, never, never give up."

Chapter 43

It Takes 21 Days to Change a Habit!

Not long ago, I enrolled in a 10-week Lean and Fit Boot Camp to get into shape. I do have a gym membership at another club but have not been using it. I needed a kick in the butt. Have you ever felt that way?

As soon as I started the boot camp, the first rule was that you were to have no alcohol for 21 days. Now, I do enjoy a glass of wine but I thought, no problem, I can do this. Was it easy? No. We had many social events to attend during those 21 days and temptation was all around me. I wanted to prove to myself that I could do it and I did. As the 10 weeks were coming to an end, I felt great. The classes were the most intense I have ever taken and the challenge they all presented is what kept me going back. Many people with whom I joined the program quit early on. As I reflect, here are some of the reasons why they quit:

- It was hard.
- It was demanding.
- There were rules.
- The instructors never let you stop pushing yourself.
- It hurt.
- I didn't feel like going.
- I got too sweaty.
- I was discouraged.

- I thought we were finished and they made us do 10 more sets.

After just 21 days, I finally started to see results and my whole attitude had changed. There was a complete increase in my energy. My goal was hard and I was refusing to give up, but at the same time I did learn a couple of lessons.

1. Adversity gave me the opportunity to look at my courage and not give up.

2. I wanted to be held accountable for my actions. I wanted to push myself to the next level in fitness and I was determined to persist through it even though it was uncomfortable.

Let's take 21 days to change a habit in our business. What habit can you change in your business over the next 21 days? Are you willing to push yourself to the next level in your business? Are you willing to hold yourself accountable to the 21-day mission? Here are a few suggestions:

- Approach 20 people face to face every day. There are so few people out there prospecting that it results in no competition for those of us who are. Have the leading edge in your industry.

- Follow up with your customers after the sale is made to ensure they are satisfied.

- Get in the habit of asking for referrals from your customers. Who do they know that could use your product or service?

- Write thank you notes by hand after the sale is made.

- Do your paperwork at the end of each day, not when it is tax time.

- Sit down the night before and set out a plan of action for the next day.

- Write down a list of three things you accomplished each day.

- Set a percentage increase to hit over the 21-day period.

- Tell someone your goal and have them hold you accountable daily.

You can implement one change every 21 days. Just imagine in the course of a year you will have changed over 17 habits!

Now, hold out your hand and squeeze it as hard as you can. That's it, squeeze it. Now squeeze it harder, come on, you can do it. Okay one more push; squeeze harder. See you did it, didn't you. Now let me ask you this, why didn't you squeeze that hard the first time I asked? The human species never pushes the limit until we are forced by some other power. The same goes in sales, we can always push harder than we are currently doing.

"Know who you are and what you really want;
there is nothing you can't do
if you put your mind to it."
John Savidis

John Savidis is a marital arts world champion. He has all the proven elements of a born champion. He trains people to their unlimited potential. During the 10-week program, there were many times John stood in front of me screaming, "Come on Lori. Do 10 more push ups." Honestly, my arms felt like they were going to fall off. They were shaking and hurting, but I pushed through and did 10 more. At the end, I felt accomplishment in that I did more than I thought I could.

What is your unlimited potential? Picture me looking you right in the eyes this very moment pushing you to reach further; "Come on, you can do it, go back out there and make one more sale, come on, I know you can do it." What is stopping you?

What habit are you going to change this month?

So here is the challenge. Starting right now, what habit are you going to change this month?

Chapter 44

Raise your Game

What is the secret to raising your game? If you had to choose players for your own team, who would you choose? Take a look at your current team now, is everyone playing to win? We all need love, energy and the support from others to succeed. It is important to realize that some people in our lives (friends, family or co-workers) can sabotage our hopes and dreams. They have the potential to completely drain us of our energy instead of helping us to build a strong business and life for ourselves.

I have coached sports teams and the most challenging was when my son was in travel hockey. The team wasn't winning so I asked the coach if I could put together an off-ice dry-land training program. I was training for my marathon at the time, so I was in my personal best physical shape I had ever been in. He asked the boys on the team what they thought and they were all for it.

At the first practice, this group of 14-year-olds thought they were in for an easy ride. After running the stairs for half an hour they were all exhausted. I kept pushing them through exercises for another half hour after which they were exhausted and realized the challenge that was ahead of them. I also entered the team into a five kilometer run to raise money to build schools in Haiti. Most of them hadn't ever run that far. One of the kids wanted to quit and said he couldn't do it. His father was the coach and ended up telling him it was okay if he didn't want to run the race. I did not agree with this, so I went to the coach myself and told him that nobody on this team was a quitter and his son was to finish like the rest of the team.

We had high energy practices and I consistently uplifted each person on the team. On the day of the race I didn't know if the coach's son would show up. He did and he was nervous. I told him that even though the others didn't show it, I could guarantee they were all nervous too. Being in a public race makes you nervous, it was natural. The team cheered him on and I told him that I would run with him and we could cross the finish line together. When his foot crossed the finish line, I felt an overwhelming urge to burst into tears of happiness but stopped myself. I high-fived him and told him how proud I was of his accomplishment. I told him that, in life, there will be times when things aren't easy, when you have to push yourself even if it hurts, but if you persevere you will get to the finish line. He commented on his last place finish after which I told him that it didn't matter where he finished, what counts is that he completed the race. A while later, some of the members of the team informed me that one of the boys cheated and took a short cut. I then told the boy I ran with that he didn't finish last and when you cheat you are only cheating yourself, or in this case, the rest of the team.

I worked with these boys for the whole season and their loosing streak turned to a winning streak. Before games, they would be skipping in the parking lot or running around the arena, they were pumped — raising their game to a new level.

What happened here for me was amazing. Before the marathon, the boys all wrote on little pieces of paper and told me to open the notes during my run. As I ran the 26.2 miles, I would open one of the papers each time I felt tired or lacking in energy. They read words of encouragement...."you can do it!", "go for it!", "we are proud of you!" The funniest one I read was when I was nearing the end of the marathon feeling parched and tired. I opened the last little piece of paper and it read, "Water is for wimps." My friend and I burst into laughter as we crossed the finish line.

A sports team is no different than a business team. You may have someone on your team who wants to quit, who wants to cheat, who talks about others behind their back or who thinks they are better than others. It may not be easy and in business you have to push yourself until it hurts, to make ends meet. In new business start ups, it takes on average three years to earn profits and have things running smoothly. That first three years hurt but, if you persevere, your hard work will be worthwhile. Make a habit to omit negative words like no, not, don't, can't or won't from your vocabulary. For example, instead of saying "I can't get a sale," reword your thoughts to "I am in the process of obtaining a sale."

Omit negative words from your vocabulary.

To raise your game you first must look at who you surround yourself with. When you have a positive team around you, you will attract more business. Who is currently on your team that needs to be removed? Who is on your team that you can encourage to do greater things? Who on your team is helping you to be the best you can be?

Build a team of friends, family, and co-workers who support you, encourage you and uplift you. Tell them your goals and ask for their support. Ask how you can support them in their life and career. Team members help each other. Pick a team of people who want to WIN.

Build a team with those who support, encourage and uplift you.

Chapter 45

Sales Are Not Always About What You Like to Do

For 20 years I have worked a booth at the Canadian National Exhibition, known as the CNE, in Toronto. This is a big fair that runs for 18 days each summer. There are rides and horse shows, entertainment, exhibitor booths and so much to see and do. I get asked all the time from friends and family why I work the fair, because it is long hours from 10AM-10PM each day. One of the only days I have missed of the CNE, I was at home sick and bothered that I was not at the booth working. Even though staying in bed all day had been wonderful, because the show is exhausting, when I am in the CNE-mode I am full ON. It isn't easy, my feet hurt and as I get older my whole body starts to ache. There is a price to pay for success and sometimes we have to do what we don't really enjoy.

There is a price to pay for success.

I can think of a million things I would rather do than commit myself to working the CNE for three-weeks each summer, however the benefits outweigh the cons and I have learned a lot over the 20 years. With the price there is a prize:

Rapport building with people you don't know.

I can't tell you how many people have told me their innermost secrets when I am serving them at my booth. I have customers who have cried, laughed, hugged me and kissed me because I took the time to listen. Building rapport generates more business. These customers will wait an hour for me to serve them when they come back year after year. They remember my children's names, my husband's name and are truly interested in me because I am truly interested in them. In sales it is important to be interested instead of interesting. I meet them once a year and am with them for maybe 20 or 30 minutes. Year after year they are repeat customers!

Stamina

Eighteen days and 12 hours of standing each day is a lot of time on your feet. Of course you get tired, but in sales and business we need to suck it up and keep on trucking day after day.

Never underestimate where your next sale will come from.

Every year we dock our boat at the marina across the street from the fair. When our children were little, if anyone asked them what I did for a living and they would say, "She works at the CNE." I always chuckled because they were so excited about going on the rides and, when they told people about that, it sounded as though I was a ride operator. This past year we were on the dock when a man from another boat asked what I did at the CNE. My 22-year-old daughter answered that I was the Ferris wheel operator. We laughed when we went back to our boat. After 5 days of seeing me getting off our 37' boat in my business suits and jewellery, they stopped me and said, "Ok we are confused, how can you afford a boat like that being a Ferris wheel operator?" I laughed and told them, that really wasn't what I did. They had spent days trying to figure out what exactly my career was. After I told them what I was doing, I ended our conversation by saying, "Never underestimate the Ferris wheel operator." Imagine all the change that they find on the ground underneath their ride, they are probably richer than you think. If I see a penny on the ground I always stop and pick it up. I always smile and put it in my pocket because I value where every penny comes from — some people do, others don't.

At a fair like this, you get people dressed in all kinds of ways. Sometimes I look around and wonder why people choose to leave the house looking as they do. As I have talked with show visitors, I find that many people are professionals who just need a day out of their business suits. They come comfortably dressed to have a fun day out. I have been surprised many times and sometimes the people who I don't think are going to buy end up spending the most.

The people who run the rides come to our booth often. They are tired, wearing their carnie shirts and sometimes they look like they can't afford much. I never underestimate their ability. They have money and love spending it on their family and loved ones who are back home waiting for them to return home. When a carnie comes to the booth, I am usually the first to walk over and ask how their day is going out on the midway. Right away we have built a common ground and we compare our long days. Then I ask them to tell me what they are looking for that day. The sale is then made without a doubt. After I pack up their purchase, I always end by telling them to send their friends, letting them know that I will be glad to help them pick out something fabulous.

My first mentor in business, Glenn Butler, taught me this lesson. He was 26-years-old and a very successful businessman. Glenn and his brother Jay, who was 28 at the time, went into a Jaguar dealership dressed in their jeans. The first salesman who was in his 40s just passed them over and didn't give them the time of day. Glenn then went to the youngest salesman in the dealership, pointed to the Jaguar car that he wanted and said, "I'll take it and I'm paying cash." I'm sure to this day the first salesman learned a very costly and valuable lesson.

You never know what you can accomplish.

Every day I get up and ask myself what is going to happen today…who am I going to meet and what new business am I going to acquire? You can't accomplish anything if you don't start your day and get to work. Success doesn't always happen immediately. At the annual CNE show, some people just browse their first time by the booth but later come back to make a purchase. If you are not as pleasant as you were the first time you met them, you can lose the sale. Success sometimes comes a little later — sometimes it comes long after the show is over when they call me back a month later. The trick is to not get discouraged and stop, just keep on pushing.

Character building.

I call the CNE my character building 18 days of the year. It builds my character and helps me to keep working on myself. As J. F. Kennedy said, "It may not be easy, it may be hard." When you do things that are difficult, it builds your character. Sometimes you have to do what you don't like to do, to make your business flourish.

You can't make a sale sitting on your butt!

If you are worried about where the next sale is, that might be your challenge. You simply have to get off your behind and make calls every single day, get out to networking events, book one-on-one appointments and be so busy that you can't see straight. This builds momentum! Every time I approach a potential customer at the CNE, it is that one more call. Sometimes I am tired, just wanting to sit on the chair and not move. However, a customer who comes up to the desk will leave if they are not approached by a salesperson. If I get up, there is a greater chance I will make the sale. Many times in the booth I will say to the other girls, "Okay, go and sell that person something." We encourage and push each other, which in turn pushes ourselves. Consistent activity is the key. Consistent activity has a

> **Consistent activity is the key.**

precession effect. If you don't practice your techniques and just wing it, you won't achieve the results you desire.

In sales, it is all about getting off your butt, you just have to make the initial decision to get up.

Stop negotiating the price for success and just start paying it. You have to want it in order to attain it.

Practice what works.

Over the years I have practiced different techniques. If I go to the large CNE show without preparation, I'll be asking for trouble. You may be smart and you may be quick on your feet, but in sales, this will only get you so far. You have to master your sales process, sales pitch and your presentation. Most importantly you must master being consistent in your business. I have built my business by doing the unglamorous stuff. To me the CNE is unglamorous because, by the end of 18 days, I am not looking as perky as I was on day one. I have bags under my eyes and customers asking me why I am limping. However, this process builds momentum and momentum builds results. Talking to one more customer, making 10 more calls, going to one more networking meeting — practicing what works. The recipe is doing the right things in massive amounts for long periods of time. It is about having the drive, determination and will to do what you don't like to do. Working the CNE every year makes me stronger, helps me with my communication skills and rapport building skills.

The recipe is doing the right things in massive amounts for long periods of time.

Do what no one else will do so you can live like no one else can live.

Momentum.

Sometimes we lose our momentum. I've seen this first-hand during the summer. Kids get out of school in June and are off for two whole months, or four if they are in university. Summer break changed the pace of everything our family did. As an entrepreneur with kids, the summer was always the toughest time of the year for me. I had to keep the momentum going over the summer. I have seen countless people stop during the summer and when the kids go back to school they have to restart their business. That is a very hard thing to do. Kids love to play and have fun and, let's face it, they aren't playing with us all day. While they are playing with their friends, work your business. Prioritize your time. Plan your day. Plan your summer. I have never missed a baseball, soccer, hockey, waterpolo, volleyball or school event in my childrens' lives and have earned a six-figure income for the past 20 years. I plan my time and, as an entrepreneur, that is the most beautiful bonus of being in business and being in sales. If I see a dress I love, I just calculate what I have to sell in order to have it — it's that easy. Build momentum in your sales.

If you have a bad day, so what?

We all have them — that's just a fact. Let go of the past and take a vow of kindness. Be kind to yourself. On days like this, I run a hot bath and just soak the tension away. I don't beat myself up because I had a bad day or low sales. I do things that make me feel good about myself so that tomorrow starts out fresh without the baggage of yesterday. We have to be our own advocates of our business. Encourage, motivate and inspire yourself to success. Remember, sales aren't always about what you like to do…

Your beliefs become your thoughts
Your thoughts become your words
Your words become your actions
Your actions become your habits
Your habits become your values
Your values become your destiny
Mahatma Gandhi

Chapter 46

Taking Initiative in Sales

When our 22-year-old daughter, Megan, came home after graduating university, she had always worked as a lifeguard during the summer. However, this summer she decided to do something fun and took a job as the beverage cart girl at a local golf course. She made unbelievable money and had a great experience. She told us about a contest called The Ultimate Canadian Cart Girl Contest which she'd heard about. She wondered if she should enter because there were only two weeks left and the contest had been open for almost three months. I told her to, "Go for it, take the initiative and just ask everyone to vote for you." As her mom, I did my part in getting friends and family to cast votes for her too. It was fun.

> **Positive actions have positive consequences.**

We learned some valuable lessons during this experience. Positive actions have positive consequences. In only two short weeks she ended up in the top three girls with the most votes. We all have a purpose, however, our action is required to fulfill our purpose. Without action, she would not have made it to the top three. She had to ask golfers to go to a web site and cast a vote for her. She made up little hand-outs with the web address on it and put up flyers in the clubhouse.

There were probably many other girls who did not take the initiative to sign up because they didn't think they would get enough votes. I believe too many people sit around waiting for things to happen. Without taking initiative we will never become the person that we were born to be and never do all the great things we are here to do. By focusing her energy on the goal, our daughter just started asking people to vote for her and also asked if they could pass the information on to their friends and family — it was a domino effect. She had a thought, then had the plan and took the action. She was focused! She figured out what she needed to do and didn't let fear get in the way. The fear of asking someone and being rejected never entered her mind.

One time she said, "What if I do all this work and don't get picked?" My answer to her was, "With your positive attitude and the action you have taken you will get the outcome you want!" Sometimes we don't always get what we want but we grow in the process and learn a lot about ourselves. The votes came in like magnets, more and more kept coming her way.

In sales, we can be a magnet to our own business. We can attract more customers than we can handle by having positive energy and taking initiative. We have unlimited potential and we can make unlimited income. All we need to do is know what we want and just go do the work. Ask, ask and ask again. Don't let the fear of rejection get in your way.

The girls that started three months previous probably lost some focus and momentum along the way, whereas my daughter had to push without stopping because she only had two weeks. Have you ever had this happen when you started a new job or new business?

There are phases we go through. In the first phase, you have uninformed unrealistic optimism. You are so excited at the beginning and your emotion shoots through the roof. You are so passionate about what you are doing. You love life and everything is perfect. The second phase is informed reality. Reality sets in and it now becomes work. You realize it isn't as easy as you thought it would be and it isn't as fun as in the past. You ask yourself, "Is this worth it?", "Can I do this?" At this point you either quit or go back to phase one to get pumped up again. If you stay here your thoughts will likely become negative about the process and you will begin to lose confidence. The third phase is hope and acceptance. You realize that there is no such thing as a perfect business and there are things you must do to move forward. The fourth phase is professionalism, you are now emotionally unattached and can operate your business and control your emotions. You treat your business as a business and realize the potential you really have.

You have to take action, get educated about the process, practice your presentation and then, and only then, you will get the results that you desire.

What is stopping you from taking initiative for a dream or vision that you have? What is the worst thing that could happen from trying something new? It may not be easy but you will learn a whole lot during the process. What phase are you in with your business right now?

The contest ended up with Megan winning the title, a 32" plasma TV for herself, one for the clubhouse and a thousand dollar travel voucher along with some other prizes. Initiative was worth the effort!

Look at your sales figures so far for the year...are they where you want them to be? If the answer is no, now is the time to take initiative, just get out there and do it.

Chapter 47

How to Rev Yourself Up in Your Business

When I had recovered from being very ill for over two weeks, I found myself with no energy. I could barely get out of bed and had to cancel some appointments — which was very difficult for me.

Once I started feeling a bit better I wanted to tackle the world again, which ended up sending me back to bed. As the doctor said, be careful and don't wear yourself out. Be patient and your strength will come back. In response to my doctor I said, "But you don't know who you are telling this to." He just laughed and said, "Lori, take it easy, it has to run its course." This is the same in sales when you want to go out and tackle the world but get knocked down with a few no's. You want to crawl back into bed again. However, the prescription is the same. Be patient and don't wear yourself out — pace yourself.

Once I had started to get stronger and really began feeling better, I started to think about how I was going to get my engine revved up again.

In sales, the key to success is to have a positive attitude. This is true in both business and in life. As we previously discussed, the victory will always go to the person with the highest energy. Initially, my attitude was not very positive because I was sick and tired of being sick. My energy was low and I wasn't winning, which was affecting my attitude. So I decided that the first thing I had to do, once

I felt better, was get up in the morning and celebrate that I was getting up. Once I had my shower, put my makeup on and got dressed for business, I was on my way. Now, some of you reading this may work from home and feel that putting on track pants or staying in your pajamas until noon is okay. The first change that I made when I started my home-based business was to get up and get dressed for business, even though I was not leaving my home. This made a big difference and this small change alone raised my energy level a few notches. If you are going to make sales calls, put on a suit. Put a mirror in front of you so that you smile at yourself. Smiles are contagious and the person on the other end of the phone will smile back at you — they can sense your mood. If you feel good about how you look, you will express this in your tone. Wouldn't you want to deal with someone who has a high energy tone of voice on the call?

I had to talk to that inner voice inside my head and realize that I was the only person who could get me going. My engine had been stopped, maybe even put in reverse. Did I want it to remain idle or did I want to rev it up? The decision was mine alone. I am the only one who can rev up my own engine. Just like in sales, we are the only ones who can make the calls, go out and do introductory calls, prospect and make contacts. We can choose to network and meet new potential customers. It's our choice!

Next, I needed to focus on my business and move from neutral to forward. I needed to know where I was going and, most of all, have the desire to head in the forward direction. I needed to set small goals at first — to call five people a day and to follow up with five people that I had left messages with. My focus needed to be action. ACTION equals SALES. If your sales aren't where they need to be, start today with an action plan and a strategy. Make your goal attainable each day.

Action = Sales

Due to my illness, my endurance was very low. I needed to fuel myself with healthy vitamins and food that would help give me positive energy. I needed to exercise my body by going for a walk and getting some fresh air. In business, if our bodies are exercised, we will have much more energy to pursue sales. Thirty minutes of exercise five days a week will keep your body moving and your mind alert.

Sales is a confronting action — primarily one where we confront ourselves, our limitations and our fears. When most people think about selling or stepping into a selling situation, they experience emotional responses automatically. That inner voice inside their head slips into overdrive and they shift into an emotional state that strips them of many of their reasoning resources. When emotions are high, our ability to think goes downhill.

Confront yourself, limitations and fears — then you can do anything!

Sales is an emotional business. We are human beings. Preparing for that emotion is the key to handling it. As we discussed earlier, learn to tell yourself positive things. This keeps you revved up! Preparation for handling questions and objections will also allow you to handle the emotional states that you encounter. The confidence you have with your polished presentation will allow you to think positively about the results you are about to achieve with your customer. All of this will serve to minimize the emotion and prepare you for successful sales!

You have to do everything you can to keep your energy up. How many days have you had where everything goes perfectly? You start the day by finding a $20 bill in your pocket, people start opening the door for you and giving you compliments — you can sell anything on these days. How about a day that's a complete disaster? Your brand new car gets scratched down the side, you break the heel of your shoe, stub your toe… We can have the attitude that "this always happens to me?" But does it? Do you really stub your toe on a daily, weekly or even monthly basis? This is the reason you have to keep your energy up. You need to be prepared all the time to handle your inner voice. Just tell it to "STOP" during adversity. You can control it!

When my illness had finally run its course, I needed to know where I was going and how I was going to get back on track. I needed to do an analysis of my business. How much business did I lose when I was sick and what did I have to do to regain that loss? I needed to put it down in dollars and also in time. This gave me a clear snapshot of where I was.

If you have built great rapport with your customers, getting business back on track is often not a problem. My customers had understood that I needed to change appointments. They told me to call them when I felt better and there was no hesitation in rebooking.

Now it was time to start having fun again. Being down and out wasn't enjoyable for me because I love to have fun. Enjoy what you are doing. Treat your customers with the respect they deserve and go into their world first. If they see you having fun at your business, they will want to deal with you. Having fun during the sales process will become contagious and in turn your sales will increase.

Go for it! Get focused and remember, the highest energy and excitement gets the victory!

Conclusion

You were born to win and, to be a winner, you must plan the action steps. Prepare to win with the skill sets of your business and expect to win with your action. The will to win is nothing without the will to prepare. You have what it takes to get where you want to go.

Take a look at the words below and write beside them if they are mindset, skill set or action words:

Enthusiastic (i.e. are you enthusiastic about what you are doing?)
Honest (i.e. are you honest in all your business transactions?)
Integrity
Dependable
Ambition
Positive Attitude
Good Self Image
Loyal
Consistent
Faith
Self Starter
Creative
Imagination
Communicator
Sense of Humor
Determined

Considerate
Loving
Desire
Listener
Fair
Healthy
Versatile
Patient
Team Player
Empathetic
Open Minded
Always smiling
Organized
Goal Setter
Hard Worker
Ethical
Appearance
Reliable

Then look at the words and analyze where you are right now.

Are these the qualities that you would like people on your team to have? Some of the qualities are mindset, where your attitude can determine where you are. Others are skill sets which can be taught and many are action steps you can take to bring your business to the next level.

When you are ready, the opportunity will be there for you. Believe in yourself and notice that the possibilities are endless. Stand in front of a mirror each morning and affirm how great you are. Visualize the results you want. Reinforce the positive qualities that you possess. Look at yourself and say your name followed by "you are a dependable, confident, reliable person." Each day pick different words of affirmation. Get on your own side and pump yourself up. Truly love yourself. The way we talk to ourselves has a definite effect on how we act towards others. The qualities I listed earlier are some qualities of the winner you were born to be. Before going to bed, do positive affirmations of your day. Have a note pad on your bedside table and list three things that went great — three positive things. It could be personal or business related. The following are often on my positive affirmation pad:

- Got 8 hours of sleep last night.
- Had family dinner together.
- Went to the gym and did a spinning class.
- Followed up with 10 clients today.
- Doubled my sales from yesterday.
- Went to a networking event and met a new prospect.
- Went on a date with my husband.
- Watched a movie with the kids.

When you learn to get along with yourself, you can get along with anyone. I have found, as a mother of two, that how I start my day has a ripple effect on my family. If I am in a great mood, the precessional effect is contagious. The same applies in business. If I am positive with my team, their attitude is also a positive one. You own the day, make the best of it!

In 1991 I heard Zig Ziggler say, "You are where you are because that is where you want to be." I wrote this saying down and have carried it in my wallet ever since. That statement is so true. If you won't lose weight, maybe you like being overweight or why wouldn't you lose weight. If you can't seem to lose weight, maybe you are lacking in motivation needed to get you going. If you are in a job you hate, maybe deep down you can't be bothered to make a change of career. If you want to increase your income but aren't making much progress, maybe you are too comfortable with what you are earning.

Here are ten essential tips:

1. The highest achievement of any human being is to serve his fellow man. I am in business to serve my clients. I must see that my customer gets what he wants. My profit is in direct proportion to the service I give. By serving others, the rewards will return to you.

2. I am responsible for everything that happens to me. If I have a problem, I caused it either by my action, reaction or inaction.

3. My professional reputation is all I have to sell and I take it seriously.

4. I would never knowingly do anything that would harm my customers, clients, friends or family.

5. I am a great communicator and a great listener.

6. I find out what my customer wants and will do my best to help him get it.

7. I offer advice based on my experience and knowledge and, if I don't know the answer, I will do what it takes to find it.

8. Everything is a sale. In business, and in life, everything is a sale. So the question is, who is going to think of a way to get the sale (mindset), who is going to present the sale (skill set) and who is going to close the sale (action step)?

9. The real winners are masters at attitude control. With your positive attitude, you will see the change in the people around you. It is contagious, they will catch what you have got.

10. By maintaining control over the way you think, feel and act, you cause good things to happen in your life. You magnetize yourself to good.

In closing, persistence is essential. You don't have to have a special gift or be a born natural with this particular trait. You first have to develop a way of thinking that will allow you to be persistent. It can be learned and you then act to develop the habit of persistence.

In life, the choice is yours. Remember, getting what you want is easier than you think. Opportunity awaits you!

go to:

www.persistencePAYS.ca

and get your bonus chapter,

"6 Secrets of Life Changing Persistence"

"Things may come to those who wait...
but only the things left by those who hustle."
Abraham Lincoln